Quilting
Around Your Home

Quilting
Around Your Home

Decorating with Quilts You Can Make

Anthony and Jeanne Jacobson

Chilton Book Company
Radnor, Pennsylvania

Published in Radnor, Pennsylvania 19089, by Chilton Book Company

Design and drawings by Anthony Jacobson
Photographs by Tim Scott
Calligraphy by Rhonda Taggart
Quilts by Anthony Jacobson unless otherwise noted

Manufactured in the United States of America

Library of Congress Cataloging-in-Publication Data

Jacobson, Anthony.
Quilting around your home : decorating with quilts you can make
Anthony and Jeanne Jacobson
p. cm.
Includes bibliographical references and index
ISBN 0-8019-8342-8
1. Quilting—Patterns. 2. Interior decoration. I. Jacobson,
Jeanne. II. Title.
TT835.J33 1993
746.9'7—dc20

93-10348
CIP

1 2 3 4 5 6 7 8 9 0   1 0 9 8 7 6 5 4 3

To

Harriett Wright

Mother of ten
Grandmother of thirty
Great Grandmother of a growing population
who inspires us all
to reach for the stars

———————————

In memory of

Crystal Palmer

a great friend and inspiration who was
taken from us much too soon

Contents

Chapter Seven Decorative Quilts 85

Chapter Eight Quilts Just for Fun! 107

Foreword

I grew up surrounded by quilts, largely because my grandmother turned them out in fine profusion. But Delpha Anne Elizabeth Taylor would no more have thought of hanging a quilt on a wall than she'd have taken a notion to leave Wewoka, Oklahoma, and go visit the queen. The quilts lay proudly on beds and humbly on porch swings, they snuggled on the sofa and in the back seat of the Studebaker. Extra blocks might be transformed into throw pillows, but there ended any flirtation with interior design. Quilts were quilts, and that was that.

Ma had more imagination, though, than a woman I once encountered who had looms for sale. At the time I was spending as much time weaving as quilting, and (neither of these activities having made me wealthy) I tried to engage this lady in some negotiations. "I'm a quilter," I said. "I could trade you a quilt for a loom." She looked at me blankly. "Why, honey," she explained, as though to a child, "I've *got* plenty of covers."

I wish that poor woman and my grandmother could read the book you're holding. They would be amazed. Anthony and Jeanne Jacobson have assembled a rich array of decorating ideas using quilts. Their concepts and designs range from simple to sophisticated, traditional to modern. Tony and Jeanne visualize a home softened, sparked, and animated by quilts. They offer a parade of ideas — table covers, wallhangings, pillows, and game boards, for instance — and then explain how to make that vision a reality. You'll find baby quilts, quilts draped over stair railings, even a quilted shower curtain.

The book begins with a basic beginner's course in quilting, then presents some eye-opening ideas for displaying the results of your work. Finally, complete instructions are given for some of the projects pictured throughout these pages.

So — if you already have some quilts, get them out and get creative around *your* home. If you don't have any, Tony and Jeanne tell you how to remedy that situation. I have more quilts than I know what to do with, but that won't stop me from starting on my favorite design in this book — the yellow pencil wall quilt. I can see it hanging over my word processor.

Margaret Dittman
Fort Worth, Texas, 1993

Preface

In our house, I am the quilter. My wife Jeanne sews her own clothes, sews crafts, and does needlework, but the quilting is all mine. I don't know if one house can handle two quilters. How could you ever keep straight whose fabric belongs to whom?

I learned to quilt when I was about ten. My grandmother, who is of a very practical nature, told me I had two hands and could make a quilt myself when I came to her once too often requesting a new one. She let me loose in her fabric closet. In this closet there were left-over fabrics from dresses she had made for my aunts while they were growing up, scraps from worn-out housedresses, and occasionally a chunk of fabric that was bought but never used. I set about choosing different fabrics and cutting out what I thought were thousands of 4″ squares. Once they were all cut out my aunt and I laid them out on the living room floor to arrange them just so. We found that a few of the pieces I had cut had black poodles on them, so we arranged them in the center. Other than that it was just a pleasant mix of fabrics of all colors.

We then picked up the squares of fabric in order by rows. My grandmother set up her sewing machine and showed me how to operate it, and I was off. I sewed all the blocks into rows and then started ed sewing the rows together in the prearranged order. Because this was my first sewing project and because the fabrics varied in their makeup, the seams didn't quite meet at the intersections. My grandmother gave me nothing but encouragement as I went along, proud of what I had accomplished.

When I had the quilt top finished we put the quilt into my great grandmother's quilting frame, which consisted of lengths of 1″ × 3″ boards with canvas strips attached to them. These were propped on the tops of the backs of four dining room chairs in the middle of the living room.

All the quilts we had when I was growing up were tied quilts, usually done with yarn. Because quilts were considered useful first and decorative second, this was an efficient way to finish them. We tied my quilt in one afternoon and my grandmother finished the edges for me. I was so proud of that quilt that I used it on my bed until it was worn out.

Looking back, I realize that aesthetically my first quilt left a lot to be desired, but it got me started on a craft I have enjoyed for 17 years since. After I graduated from college, I decided to take a stab at hand quilting. Not knowing just how complicated hand quilting might be, I decided to start with a small wall quilt.

My grandmother had never done any hand quilting while I was around, so I taught myself how to do it. Later, as I got deeper into quilting, I realized that the way I quilted was not the method used by most quilters. I had gone too far to turn back, however, so I still use an up-and-down stitch instead of a running stitch. It gives a much different look to the stitch, which I like.

After my good luck with the wall quilt I designed a quilt for my newborn niece. The fact that I had drawn templates for my grandmother combined with my experience as a graphic designer inspired me to create my own designs. That first baby quilt I designed for my niece was a clown teddy bear—I love clowns and my sister-in-law collects teddy bears. Since then, my favorite quilts have been the baby quilts. However, I don't believe that a baby's things should be all pastels and my baby quilts aren't. I've done a trapunto bunny climbing through quilt blocks, a farmer teddy bear, and pink polka-dot elephants, which made the lattice work in the quilt sag. It's getting harder to come up with creative ideas, but I always seem to.

Along with thinking of new ideas for baby quilts, I put my creative juices to work on other uses for quilts and quilted items. Jeanne pointed out to me, after we were married, that we had only so many beds and they already had quilts on them. So, I knew I had to find other uses for the quilts I was making or find something else to occupy my time. First I worked on wall quilts for some of the spaces where we lacked artwork. Not only have quilts finally gained acceptance for the works of art that they are; they are also good at filling large areas.

My grandmother didn't quite know what to think of my wall quilts at first because she is more practical when it comes to quilts.

Making baby quilts can be a lot of fun. This quilt combines a traditional quilt block pattern with a twist. Courtesy of Paige Morgan Glassman.

She thought that I had lost it when I told her of my plans to do a quilted shower curtain. I can only imagine what thoughts will go through her head when she looks at some of the unusual quilts in this book.

So, take those quilts out of the bedroom and be creative. Quilts belong wherever you want and can bring lots of enjoyment. Put them on tables, on shelves, over chairs, in windows, and outdoors. No matter what your needs or decorating style, whether it be Victorian, Arts and Crafts, or Art Deco, quilts can be used. They are as appropriate for ultramodern decor as for the country look. Just as painting styles vary so do quilting styles. Let creativity be your guide and quilt away!

Anthony Jacobson

Using ripstop nylon you can make quilted covers for your metal patio chairs. These will hold up under normal conditions, but they should be brought in during severe weather.

Acknowledgments

We would like to thank those who have supported us through the creation of this book. Most especially our gratitude goes to our grandmothers, who taught us an appreciation for the art of quilting. Through the years we have also had the support and encouragement of our parents, who have urged us to go after our dreams.

This book would not be possible without the talent of our photographer, Tim Scott. We appreciate his time and effort and his family's patience as we monopolized his weekends.

A special thanks to the wonderful people from the following manufacturers who sent quilts: Alexander Henry Fabrics; Concord Fabrics; Fabric Traditions; Hi-Fashion Fabrics, Inc.; Kona Bay Fabrics; and V.I.P. Fabrics. Also, thanks to Ann Boyce for putting us is touch with these people and Debra Wagner for sending some of her own quilts to be photographed.

The following people were gracious enough to let us come into there homes to do the photography: Joseph and Mary Ciurlino, Mike Ippoliti, Pam Lounsbury, Gene and Dina Mancini, Rick and Denise Moore, Pierre Robert, Joe and JoAnne Romanek, and Troy and Beth Vozzella.

We thank those people who supplied us with materials to be used in the photo shoots: Cindy Scott for two vintage quilts; South for the Winter Antiques for the use of glassware and dinnerware; Dina Mancini for her original Christmas houses; Mim McDevitt, Lauren Moore, and Cameron Vozzella for miscellaneous props used throughout the book.

Other people were patient and understanding as they helped us learn word processing. We wish to thank Cass Latzko, Dave Secan, and Susan Nejako for their computer know-how.

Quilting
Around Your Home

Introduction

Many of our earliest childhood memories involve quilts. Perhaps Grandma had a favorite quilt at her house that she wrapped around you while you snuggled on her lap. Or maybe you had one on your bed and remember being fascinated by the colors, fabrics, and patterns. Some of our grandmothers and/or mothers quilted, which evokes memories of quilt frames set up in the living room and thousands (or so it seemed) of different, tiny pieces of fabric organized into neat piles on the dining room table, just waiting to be sewn together. Maybe the memory is of burrowing down as far as you could into your quilt on a snowy winter morning, not wanting to budge, even though Mom and Dad were calling "Breakfast is ready!" from the kitchen.

Possibly the experience is more recent, as in your accidentally discovering a pieced but unfinished quilt top found in an old pillowcase tucked into a back corner of a closet. Or while you strolled through the aisles of a flea market or antiques show, you spotted the perfect old quilt for your family room hanging casually over a backdrop in one of the booths. We could go on and on, but a common thread (no pun intended) holds these memories together — the feeling of nostalgia inspired by a quilt.

Using vintage quilts to decorate can give your home a personal touch. Bed quilt by Eunice Meads; wall quilt and pillow embroidery by Harriett Wright, quilted by the author.

Memories like these become more and more precious as we grow older. Nowadays, more people move from city to city as the job market or business climate changes. Gone, for the most part, are jobs where you begin and end your career with one company. Now, if a

Fig. I-1. Two variations on the same quilt pattern.

better opportunity arises, people are less hesitant to move on. Life is much less stable and much more tumultuous, and therefore more stressful. Perhaps that is one reason why in the past decade quilt collecting has undergone a tremendous surge in popularity. In a world that doesn't seem as secure as it used to be and is often a little frightening, what could better help bring a feeling of warmth and permanence to your home than a quilt?

Uses for quilts have changed as the world has. In Grandma's day a quilt was purely a practical item: functional (as a bed cover), utilitarian (to use scraps of fabric too good to throw away, but too small for anything else), and most of all necessary (for warmth). The advent of modern heating systems and electric blankets have eliminated the need for quilts as a provider of warmth. Mail-order catalogs and department stores are overflowing with beautiful comforters and linens to outfit your bed, no matter your budget. Still, many people

have chosen to have a quilt on their bed, while others hang them on the wall as artwork in a more public area of the house. Others may toss one over a sofa as a throw, or even spread a large quilt across the dining room table as a cover.

How to Use This Book

We have intended this book to be used for inspiration: whether to bring quilts into your life if none are there now or to use quilts you already own in ways you may not have previously considered. Included in *Quilting Around Your Home* are projects for you to try, some less difficult for the beginning quilter, as well as ones to challenge those with more advanced skills. Many of the projects are new interpretations of traditional patterns, with the new look coming from using different fabrics or color combinations. There are several original designs as well.

The first part of the book provides a basic background on the

history of quilts and quilting, how to care for and display your quilts, quilt terminology and quilting techniques, and color theory and fabric selection suggestions. Many other excellent resources for this information already exist, a few of which we have listed in the Bibliography. The middle chapters suggest creative uses for quilts throughout the house and how you can alter the look of a room by either changing or adding quilts. The remaining chapters consist of detailed directions, accompanied by photographs and drawings, for projects to make, from the practical to the whimsical. Templates are included at the back of the book.

Quilting Around Your Home is a collection of ideas of how to pull the quilts off the bed and spread the quilts throughout the house . . . and beyond. The possibilities are endless—all you need is a little imagination and a quilt or two!

PART I
A Quilting Primer

CHAPTER ONE

Quilt Terminology

Most readers of this book will have some degree of familiarity with sewing terminology but may not feel as comfortable with the terminology used commonly in quilting. Many sewing terms overlap into quilting and vice versa. Following is a brief overview of the terms most often used in quilting, which will be a helpful tool for the beginning quilter as well as a quick reference for those who have quilted before. Wherever possible we have included the history of the term being defined to help in understanding the context in which it is used.

A *quilt* can be defined as consisting of three layers; two layers are of cloth with a layer of batting "sandwiched" between. The entire "sandwich" is then stitched or tied together and the edges finished.

Traditionally, the top and back of the quilt are of fabric woven from fibers and the batt, or middle, layer is nonwoven, that is, of fibers such as polyester, cotton, or wool. In the not-so-distant future, these layers could be constructed of paper, plastic, or anything else a creative quilter combines.

Appliqué—A piece of fabric, often in an intricate pattern, sewn with a blind stitch onto another piece of fabric.

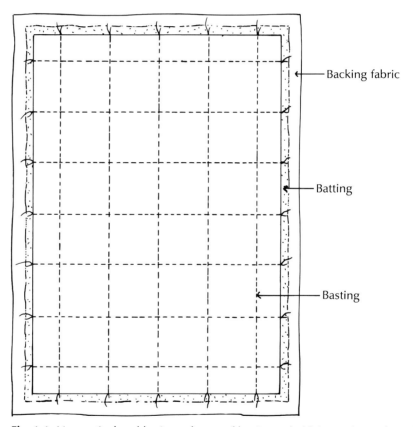

Fig. 1-1. Use vertical and horizontal rows of basting to hold the quilt together while quilting.

Backing—The bottom, or underside, of a quilt. The backing can also be pieced, and if so is usually in a nondominant pattern.

Basting—a loose running stitch used to secure the three quilt layers together to prevent one layer from shifting during the quilting process. Basting does not follow any pattern, is removed upon completion of the quilting phase, and is not considered a permanent stitch.

Batting—The nonwoven middle layer in a quilt. Batts made of polyester are most commonly used in contemporary quilts, but cotton

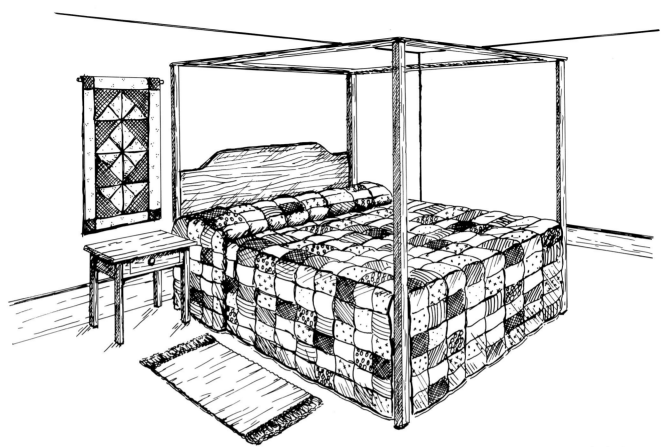

Fig. 1-2. Notches have been taken out of the bottom corners of this bedspread-length quilt to allow it to drape between the bedposts.

and sometimes wool are also used. Wool is found most often in very old quilts, and in the nineteenth century, it was popular to use cotton batting when cotton became widely available.

Bedspread—A bed cover similar to a coverlet, but a bedspread covers the bed and drops to the floor.

Bias—Fabric bias is the 45-degree angle to which it is woven. Bias strips stretch no matter how tightly woven, which is helpful in binding a quilt, especially one with curved edges.

Binding—The fabric edge finishing on a quilt, most often done on the fabric bias.

Block—A unit, usually square, of plain fabric, pieced fabric, or with an appliqué design, combined with additional blocks to create a quilt

top. Although never widely popular in Europe, the block method has developed into an art form in the United States, and is the most common form used in American quilting.

Border—The outside edge of most quilts, directly inside the binding. A border can be plain, pieced, or with an appliqué and of any width.

Chroma—The purity or saturation of a color. Used in the Munsell system of color notation.

Contrast—The difference between light and dark colors. The use of high-contrast color fabrics in a quilt, such as dark green and white, will give a much different look than would two similar colors of dark green.

Coverlet—A partial bed cover that does not drop to the floor. Most

quilts are done as coverlets, due to the size constraints of a typical quilt frame.

Crazy Quilt—A quilt pieced from odd and various pieces of fabric onto a background fabric. Often the seams are embroidered in a decorative stitch for an elegant finished effect. Crazy quilts were immensely popular during the Victorian era of the late nineteenth century.

Drop—The portion of a quilt that is along the sides of a bed. If using a quilt on a shelf or table, it is the portion hanging over the edge.

Echo Quilting—A quilting method that begins by quilting around a pattern and repeating the pattern out toward the border of a quilt. The effect is similar to the ripple effect on a lake or pond.

A hot air balloon was used in this picture quilt. Hobbies and other interests can give you inspiration for quilt designs. Courtesy of Earl and Deloris Jacobson.

Fig. 1-3. The center block in this quilt has been set on point.

Grain – The direction of the threads used in fabric.

Hue – The name of a color. Also used in the Munsell system of color notation.

In-the-Ditch Quilting – A method of stitching as close as possible to the seams in a quilt.

Lap Quilt – A small quilt, sometimes called a "lap robe," used while seated. The size can vary but is normally around 48″ × 60″.

Loft – The thickness of the batting sheet or batting blanket.

Medallion – A quilt where the main focus is in the center of the quilt top. The design of the quilt builds from the inside and fans out. Medallion quilts were very popular in England in the late eighteenth century, where many fine examples still exist.

On Point – A quilt displayed at a 45-degree angle. Quilt blocks can also be done on point, in which the blocks are tilted at a 45-degree angle within the square or rectangle of the quilt top.

Outline Quilting – Quilting approximately ¼″ around a pattern or along a seam.

Pictorial Quilting – Quilting in shapes that are representative images, for example, leaves or animals.

Piece – The small units of fabric to be combined into a quilt block.

Piecing – The process of combining small pieces of fabric together into blocks.

Quilt Frame – A structure used for holding a quilt flat and taut for quilting.

Quilting – The act of sewing the quilt layers together.

Rod Pocket — A strip of fabric stitched onto the back of a finished quilt. A hanging rod can be pushed through the pocket to hang the quilt.

Running Stitch — A stitch used to sew the quilt layers together. The running stitch was not common in Europe until recently, but it was used extensively in early American quilting, and is still being used today.

Scrap — Small pieces of fabric, leftover from quilting and sewing projects. A scrap quilt is a way to use leftover bits of fabric from other projects, and is an excellent composition challenge to the quilter.

Shade — The addition of black to a pigment to darken the color.

Stencil — Used to trace the quilting pattern onto the quilt top. A stencil can also be used to create painted patterns or images on the fabric, which may then be quilted around.

Strip Piecing — Stitching together pieces, usually of the same size, in rows and then joining the rows together to form the quilt top.

Template — The pattern used to trace around to mark the fabric for cutting out or quilting the quilt pieces. Templates can be metal, paper, plastic, wood, etc., and can be purchased or created from everyday household items.

Tie (or Tied) — A fast method of joining the quilt layers together. Tying with a knot (or in some cases a bow) is used instead of quilting by machine or hand.

Tint — The addition of white to a pigment to lighten the color.

Tone — The addition of gray to a pigment color.

The middle section and borders were created by using a stencil and fabric paint. More intricate designs can be accomplished by using stencils rather than traditional appliqué techniques.

Top — the right, or dominant, side of a quilt. The top is usually, but not always, the side with the most elaborate pattern.

Trapunto — A quilting method by which a small cut is made into the back of a section and then stuffing is added into the space. Trapunto gives dimension to the finished quilt.

Value — The lightness and darkness of any color.

CHAPTER TWO

History of Quilts and Quilting

Gaily colored, multipieced calico quilts created during the Depression, or the simple, profoundly elegant Amish quilts from Lancaster County, Pennsylvania are what most of us imagine when we think of a quilt. In America, as well as in other countries around the world, examples of quilts go back much further in time. Nearly every country and culture has a form of quilting among its creative art forms. Decorating with quilts is not a new concept, nor is it a strictly American phenomenon.

One of the earliest examples of a quilt is shown on a sculptured figure residing in the British Museum. The figure dates from 3400 B.C. and a definite patchwork pattern is visible on the robe of the figure. Quilts and patchwork may go back even further, as many quilt historians believe. Although there is not definite proof, the chances are good that as long as there have been weavers, some form of patchwork and quilting has existed.

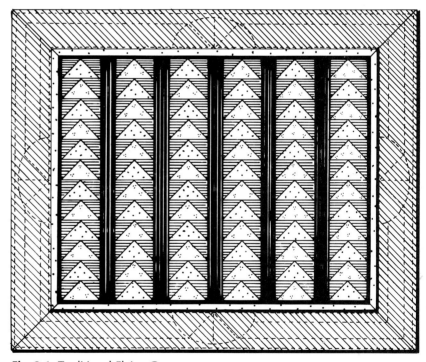

Fig. 2-1. Traditional Flying Geese pattern.

European Quilts

Pieced silk panels, dating from the sixth through nineth centuries, have been discovered in India, and an example of fourteenth century stuffed work (most commonly known as *trapunto*) has been located in Italy. How the Indian pieces were actually used has not been established, and in many ways it is not as important as the fact the pieces survived at all. Silk is a fabric on which age and environmental conditions can wreak considerable havoc; it easily deteriorates to the point of disintegration. The climate in India, with its constant heat and humidity, not to mention the intense rainy season, is not ideal for delicate textiles, much less antique textiles 15 centuries old.

The Italian trapunto piece depicts scenes from the life of the legendary knight Tristram, and sections of this quilt reside in the Palazzo Davanzati in Florence and the Victoria and Albert Museum in London. Italy, where the decorative arts are so much a part of life, can also lay claim as the source of inspiration behind the development of many modern quilt patterns. The decorative tile patterns in the great cathedrals and palazzos have provided many quilters with the initial concepts that have evolved over the years into quilt patterns such as the Tumbling Blocks and Flying Geese.

When quilts were actually introduced to Europe has never been pinpointed, but possibly it was through the travels and experiences of the Crusaders. The Arab soldiers these warriors fought had a definite advantage. Instead of heavy armor, the Arab soldiers were outfitted with quilted jackets topped by lightweight chain mail, which made them much more mobile, on horseback or on foot, and gave them a decided advantage. This concept in "modern" military apparel was brought back from the Middle East by the Crusaders to their European homelands.

As quilting evolved in Europe, another form became popular. By 1600, Europeans, especially in France, were able to acquire brightly colored and heavily patterned cotton fabrics produced in India. The quilters would cut out and around sections of these cotton fabrics, turn the edges under, and arrange the pieces on top of a larger piece of fabric. When a suitable or

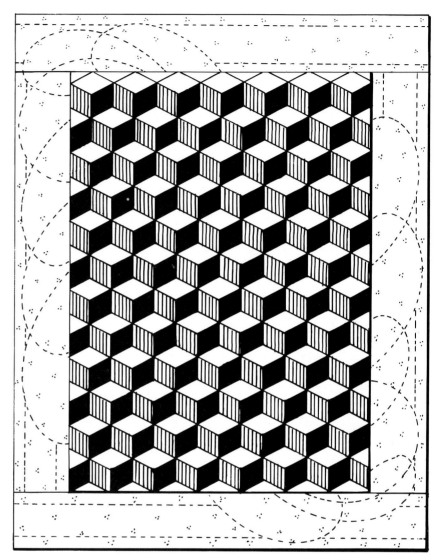

Fig. 2-2. This quilt was made from the Tumbling Blocks pattern.

pleasing pattern was arranged, the pieces were then appliquéd with a blind stitch onto the quilt top. This form of quilting became known as *broderie perse*, which comes from the French word for Persian embroidery. This form of quilting was popular for more than 100 years. By the end of the eighteenth century European fabric mills were technologically advanced enough that their fabrics were the equivalent of the imported Indian cottons commonly being used. Broderie perse remained popular in Europe, especially the Tree of Life pattern.

English Quilting

Examples of English quilting date from the early seventeenth century. These pieces exhibit extremely sophisticated composition of forms and colors, piecing techniques, and quilting methods. Patchwork and quilted bed hangings and covers were considered valuable items in the great homes of England, as indicated by the large and detailed number of examples listed in wills or house inventories over the centuries. Unfortunately, most of the items listed do

This Oriental quilt was constructed using broderie perse techniques to create the fans. Quilt by Ann Boyce. Courtesy of Kona Bay Fabrics.

not survive today which proves they were very much used.

Quilts were also heavily used in homes much smaller than the country estates of the aristocracy. In these homes, quilts were needed for their warmth. The methods of quilting were not as elaborate as those of the quilts found in the great homes. Patchwork quilts were a thrifty use of leftover fabric scraps and old, worn clothing. The results of these efforts are often referred to as English cottage quilts. But women weren't the only quiltmakers. Wonderful quilts were also done by

men, especially after one of England's many wars. Soldiers recovering from war injuries or illnesses found quilting to be an excellent way to recuperate and still contribute to their household's welfare. Children also began quilting at an early age, so the cottage quilt can truly be called a family affair.

In the early decades of the eighteenth century, chintz fabrics became easily and readily available in England, and the broderie perse type of quilting, which was all the rage on the European continent, became just as popular in Britain.

The English used remnants of these chintz fabrics, in florals and patterns, in quilting for almost 200 years. Many of these quilts still exist and are beautiful examples of composition and the quilter's skill at appliqué.

Other types of quilting were also popular in England during the eighteenth century. Quilts using cord quilting and trapunto have been found. By the 1860s, the Victorian era was in full force in England with quilts and quilting still as popular as ever. During the nineteenth century, additional quilt methods or "fads," such as crazy quilting, tumbling block patchwork, and the use of silk and taffeta in quilts, were introduced and explored by avid quilters.

Quilts in the British Isles followed similar styles and patterns, but there were regional differences. For example, in northern England and in Wales, most quilting methods were used, with the region's most dominant form being whole cloth quilted work. Elaborate quilting patterns were much more prevalent than pieced work or appliqué and were intended to showcase the quilter's stitching skills.

Commemorative quilts, especially those noting or recognizing a royal event, were common through the mid-nineteenth century. This highly prized quilt form was particular to England; European quilters very seldom crafted commemorative quilts. Commemorative quilts were just one example of the pride the English held for their monarchy and their country in the Victorian era when England was one of the world's most powerful countries.

Crazy quilts also became extraordinarily popular in Victorian England. Crazy quilts were one of the first English quilt methods to heavily utilize silk, taffeta, satin, brocade, and velvet, fabrics that came into vogue during Queen Victoria's reign. Victorian England introduced to the world the concept of specific uses for each room of the house. As a result Victorian homes had many small rooms, with separate and distinct functions. It was popular to have a formal parlor with elaborate furnishings, fabrics, and decorative items, and crazy quilts, with their decorative fabrics and embroidery, were perfect additions to the room. Unfortunately, the fabrics used are fragile and many of the quilts produced during

Fig. 2-3. Anything goes when it comes to crazy quilts.

this period have not survived or, if they do, are in less-than-mint condition.

Template-pieced quilts were another uniquely English method. Paper pieces, or templates, were cut out in the finished size and quantity needed for the entire quilt top. The fabric pieces were then basted onto the paper template. To assemble the quilt, the pieces were arranged in the desired pattern and joined together by an overhand stitch. This method of piecing allows for extremely straight and accurate seams with virtually invisible stitching. In paper template piecing, often called English piecing, the paper isn't always removed from the quilt top before quilting. Studying the remains of paper in the quilt seams is an interesting way to trace the quilt's origins and history.

By the twentieth century, quilts and quilting in England had fallen out of favor and very few quilts were produced. In the 1970s there was a renaissance of quilting that has remained to the present day.

American Quilting

Quilting in the colonies was a different endeavor than quilting in Europe. The colonists faced certain situations, which necessitated a different approach to the art of the quilt: These early pioneers used their quilts as a means of warmth rather than for any intended decorative purpose.

Very few quilts from the late seventeenth century or even the early eighteenth century still exist. Those that do remain are simple and serviceable, without much color or patchwork and with only basic stitching. For the most part, quilts from this time period wore out from daily use and were discarded. The only record of many of these are, as with early English quilts, in wills and household inventories from the period.

Quilts that did survive from the eighteenth century had a heavy influence from the European quilting and needlework traditions. The settlers, for the most part, came from different locations in Europe and brought their various quilt and stitchery forms from their homelands. This was the foundation on which the new American quilt tradition was established.

Examples of appliqué, piecing, and embroidery were all brought into the New World, as well as more specialized, regional pieced patterns, such as Tumbling Blocks. Because thread and cloth were scarce and precious, the English quilting method using a back stitch to quilt was quickly replaced by the running stitch, which used only half the amount of thread and saved a tremendous amount of time.

Fabric was not as readily available in America as it was in Europe during the same time period. The selections available were not only limited, they were also expensive due to being imported through England and were heavily surcharged and taxed. Eventually, this situation eased, particularly after the Revolutionary War, and America began to import fabric directly.

When imported fabrics became more reasonably priced and widely available, quilting in America began to bloom quickly. Quilting was fast becoming one of the few expressive art forms for American women, rich and poor alike. For the

pioneer woman, who moved with her family when the westward expansion began, the social event of a quilting bee was considered compensation for a hard, rather bleak life. Quilting bees were practical and social all-day events, where one gathered with friends to create a new piece. Wealthier women in the cities of the East and in the South used quilting as a means of showing off their sewing and embroidery prowess to friends. Quilting bees were just as important to the women of the cities as they were to the women on the prairies.

The method of creating quilts by patchwork was also expanded upon by the early American quilter. Early on, patchwork quilts were frugal uses of old worn-out work clothes and scrap fabric. Eventually the patchwork quilt became a work of art. A truly American method of quilting is the block method, which evolved from the patchwork quilt, and was a fast, thrifty, and easily transportable way to assemble a quilt. By the 1830s, with materials becoming more available, the patchwork quilt from ragbag scraps was slowly easing into a planned

Fig. 2-4. This quilt pattern is formed by blocks pieced together with lattice strips and setting blocks between them.

quilt from fabrics purchased solely for that purpose.

Another direction in American quilting was developing around the same time. The Amish were developing their own tradition of deep, intense solid colors, with impeccable piecing and quilting which was usually, but not always, done in the block method. Older Amish quilts are desirable as collectibles, due to the rich, warm, and vibrant colors found in the hand-dyed cloth. Hand-dyed cloth is hard to recreate commercially, and the use of this cloth gives Amish quilts much of their individual character. These quilts are done by a people who have minimal contact with the modern world, for they live with no electricity, telephones, radios, or televisions, and their quilts reflect this. Patterns such as Tumbling Blocks and Ocean Waves reflect their ability to find beauty in common, everyday things and to express it creatively.

Generally, the quilts produced by the Amish who settled in the Midwest have a much more daring use of color, pattern, and composition than quilts produced by the Amish of Lancaster County area of Pennsylvania. The Midwestern Amish were more isolated from other Amish, and their quilts, while still reflecting the same general qualities exhibited in the eastern quilts, show much more influence in colors and fabrics from "the English," as the non-Amish are called.

The European and English quilt styles were expanded upon in the nineteenth century. Broderie perse became so popular that new

This quilt was commercially made in a traditional Amish pattern called Ocean Waves. A large quilt works well as a backdrop and adds color to the room.

imported chintz fabrics were purchased and cut apart specifically for a quilt top. The appliqué concept was further investigated by American quilters, who created their own patterns. Patterns were most often created from individual components, such as flowers, buds, and leaves, and were combined to create the overall design. This derivative of appliqué still works beautifully with the block method of piecing quilts.

During the mid-1800s it was apparent that the same quilt patterns were showing up in various regions of the country. Some form of a quilter's network was in existence to communicate these patterns, although nothing on paper exists to give positive proof. The late nineteenth century brought about many changes to improve the quality of life for Americans, and one of them was free rural mail delivery from the Postal Service. Transfer of patterns, and availability of supplies and fabrics, became much easier (which makes the earlier movement of the various patterns around the region all the more curious and interesting). Another change included the invention of the sewing machine for the home. The sewing machine opened an entirely new avenue for the quilter, which is still being explored today.

Late Victorian America also caught the crazy quilt "bug," with approximately the same results as in England. Some very lovely crazy quilts, with beautiful embroidery were produced. Around the turn of the century, when the crazy quilt started to die out as a popular pattern, quilts and quilting began to be less popular. With the onset of the Depression, however, quilting made a definite comeback. Many wonderful quilts exist and are even

still in use from this time period. During the darkest economic period in American history, old quilt patterns, as well as new, were being constructed from bright, cheerful, and upbeat colors. Quilters in the 1930s as well as those who used these quilts, would be certain to get a momentary lift when around these constructions. Quilting bees again became popular as before — for social as well as practical reasons. Juried quilt exhibits at county and state fairs were very popular as well, with entire competitions often being on one pattern alone.

After the Depression and World War II, quilting again experienced a serious decline in popularity. Quilts were still being produced, but not in the numbers seen previously. With the postwar economy booming, personal incomes rising, and technology advancing by leaps and bounds, a handmade item, especially one as time-consuming as a pieced, patchwork quilt, was deemed passé. In the 1940s, 1950s and 1960s, ready-made was in and handmade was out . . . and in a big way.

The 1970s brought about a renewed interest in quilts and quilting. Several major quilt exhibitions helped to renew an interest in and an appreciation of quilts, especially as an art form. A quilt exhibit originating at the Whittney Museum in New York in the early 1970s, and organized by Jonathan Holstein and others, has been attributed to the resurgence of interest in quilts in the United States. After the exhibit toured the world for four years, interest in quilts in England and the rest of Europe was stirred also.

As we move into the last decade of the twentieth century, quilts and quilting in the United States, as well as in other countries, are as popular as ever. Quilting guilds and societies are continuing the quilt tradition in America, often with long waiting lists of quilters and would-be quilters interested in joining.

One of the largest and most poignant examples of quilts in the late 1980s is the AIDS Memorial quilt, which was first unveiled in Washington, D.C., as a remembrance to those who died of AIDS. The quilt can truly be called one of the largest commemorative quilts of its kind, which unfortunately, is still being added onto.

As we approach the twenty-first century, quilting in the United States is continuing to thrive. With new techniques such as machine quilting as well as the time-honored method of hand piecing and quilting, quilts will remain well in the forefront of American creative arts for years to come.

Fig. 2-5. Like many examples of Hawaiian quilting, echo quilting has been used to accentuate the appliqué design.

Quilts in Other Continents

Quilt traditions are found not only in Europe and North America. Many cultures in Asia, Africa, and South America have forms of quilted or quiltlike fabric constructions as a native art form. Several of the examples push the definition of a quilt to the limit but are included because certain aspects of their method of construction can be identified as similar to the ones described as a quilt.

In Japan, artisans use a traditional quilting method called *sashiko*. A sashiko quilt is a whole cloth quilt and is quilted with multiple strand thread, with only four to six stitches in each inch of fabric. The traditional color combination is white thread on an indigo blue background, but dark or multicolored thread on a light background

is also common. Sashiko quilting's origins are simple and functional: Farmers and other country people would stitch fabric together to create simple cloth garments that were comfortable as well as warm.

The tropical Hawaiian Islands also has a quilt tradition. In the mid-nineteenth century, missionaries were assigned to bring Christianity to the islands, and in an effort to "civilize" the native women, the missionary wives taught quilting and sewing to high-ranking Hawaiian women. The notion of doing any work of this sort was, to say the least, a novelty to these aristocratic women, but very little time elapsed before both a unique and striking quilting style was developed. The best description of this purely Hawaiian style would be a "paper

snowflake" style of appliqué. Hawaiian-type quilts consists of a solid-colored top, with intricate cutouts, which are then reverse appliquéd to a contrasting background and quilted heavily. The sources of inspiration for Hawaiian quilts are diverse: Victorian fancy paper cutting, traditional quilting and appliqué techniques, and native patterns normally applied to tapa cloth, a thin, delicate cloth beaten out of tree bark.

Another similar form of quilting, also found in a warm climate, comes from the country of Laos. *Hmong* quilts are not in reality quilted to finish the piece but they do employ extensive appliqué work similar in construction to Hawaiian quilts. Hmong quilts consist of a cutout top reverse appliquéd to a highly contrasting color backing fabric, but the similarities end there. The appliqué pattern is much less intricate and fanciful than Hawaiian quilts, and no middle batt layer or actual quilt stitches are used. In Hmong quilts precise, nearly invisible stitching is found and the composition is one of complete symmetry and balance.

On the African continent, a form of appliqué quilting exists, created solely for symbolic reasons. *Dahomey* appliqué has been used in West Africa for centuries as a pictorial record of outcomes of battle and the exploits of great warriors. These were usually in the form of banners, and in combination with traditional songs comprised a major and important role in the culture of the people of West Africa. Today replicas of the original banners can be found for sale in African markets. Although the tribesmen no longer use them as extensively as before, the ones for sale are a continuation of a proud tradition.

In South America, both Panama and Chile have quilts within their native craft traditions. In Panama the *mola* is somewhat similar to Hmong quilting, with a cutout top appliquéd to a contrasting back or bottom layer. The appliqué stitch is not as dense in the mola and the patterns, at least the early ones, are simple and abstract. Later molas have become more intricate, but the traditional method of construction and color choices has remained constant. The Chilean *arpillera* is a pictorial fabric collage quilt, closer in intent to the Dahomey pieces of Africa, but with more applied surface relief and less appliqué. The arpillera is often used to express the viewpoint of the craftsperson, and many express strong political sentiments in their creations.

Whether created for warmth, decorative embellishment, political propaganda, or as a reason for social interaction, quilts and the people who create them, are as widespread as they are diverse. Quilts are an art form and are reflective of economic, social, historical, or political influences throughout the world.

CHAPTER THREE

Quilting Basics

Constructing your own quilt, from fabric purchase to bound and finished piece, is a step-by-step process with considerable preparation required. Don't panic—the whole process is easily broken into steps and each step can be attacked and completed one at a time. Creating your own quilt can be an immensely satisfying and, most of all, a fun undertaking.

Basic Equipment

The first thing to consider before you start your quilt is the equipment you will need to construct the quilt. A rule of thumb is to purchase the best tools, fabrics, and supplies you can afford. The better quality you buy, the longer the items will last and the better your finished project will be. Like anything else you buy, you get what you pay for. A "too-good-to-be-true" price on a sewing machine may be just that, especially if your machine spends most of your quilting time in the repair shop. Or inexpensive fabrics may be a great bargain, but if the colors bleed or fade immediately, they are not worth any price.

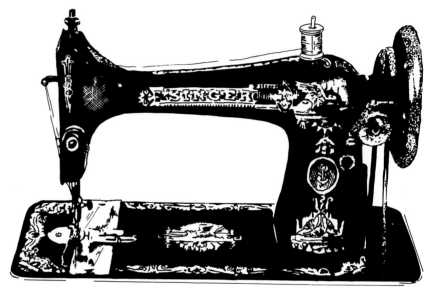

Fig. 3-1. Even a treadle sewing machine in good working order will work for your quilting projects.

Sewing Machine

One of the largest and most expensive pieces of equipment you will purchase, if you choose to machine piece and quilt, is a sewing machine. The machine doesn't need to be fancy, a good, dependable straight stitch is the only stitch required to construct most quilts. Another useful machine stitch is the zigzag stitch, used for machine appliqué or embroidery. Most sophisticated machines have other decorative stitches that also can be used in quilting and add a new dimension to a quilt.

Keeping the machine in proper working order is extremely important. Frequent cleaning and adjustment of your sewing machine will keep it running smoothly. When cleaning your machine change the needle, too. Needles need to be changed frequently; a dull, nicked, or bent needle will cause sewing problems such as skipped stitches, breaking thread, and incorrect stitch tension. Be careful to use the correct size needle for the type of fabric you are sewing. Most needle packages and sewing stores have general recommendations for what type of needle to use with what fabric.

Scissors and Rotary Cutters

Scissors and rotary cutters also need to be of good quality. If treated correctly, a good pair of scissors will last for many years. A quilter needs several different types of scissors, for different types of jobs, but all scissors need to be sharp and in good repair. Dull scissors, or ones that are falling apart, can make cutting fabric difficult and inaccurate. The most common scissors used by quilters for cutting fabrics are dressmaker's shears. These scissors are large and have a bent handle specifically engineered to easily and effortlessly cut fabrics. Dressmaker's shears come in different sizes and lengths, so you can choose the one most comfortable for you. Choosing a pair of scissors may take some time because you may have to try several before finding the right one for your hand. Remember, to use your dressmaker's shears *only* on fabric. The worst thing to do with a sharp, precisely set pair of fabric scissors is to cut paper or, even worse, cardboard. In our house we have kitchen scissors, paper scissors, and sewing scissors, and never the twain shall meet . . . and if they do, the consequences are drastic.

Because of the size of dressmaker's shears, it is recommended that you purchase a pair of embroidery scissors for use when clipping curves, snipping the ends of threads, or any other precise trimming work. The newest type of scissors to hit the quilting scene are appliqué scissors. These scissors have

a wide flange on one blade, which makes cutting through sheer, delicate fabrics, as well as cutting small curves, a much easier process.

A recent and immensely popular addition to the line of cutting tools used in quilting is the rotary cutter. Rotary cutters employ an extremely sharp round blade in a plastic housing. In combination with a proper cutting ruler and cutting mat, cutting square, triangular, and any straight-edge quilt pieces is a much less tedious process. Many manufacturers market rotary cutters and replacement blades, and they are a wonderful time- and effort-saving device. When purchasing a rotary cutter, be sure to buy one with a safety shield.

Fig. 3-2. Rotary cutters like this one can come in very handy when cutting out multiples of the same piece.

A cutting mat is necessary to protect the cutting surface when using a rotary cutter. The matts are usually constructed of self-healing plastic with a 1″ (or other dimension) measured grid imprinted on the surface. Cutting mats come in many sizes, ranging from 8½″ × 11″ to large enough to cover a small table.

You will also need accurate cutting rulers. The higher quality rulers have a grid marked on the entire ruler, which makes measuring easier as well as faster. These rulers are usually constructed of Plexiglas ⅛″ thick, which will most accurately help you guide the rotary cutter.

Again, you get what you pay for; inexpensive cutters may break

or malfunction and poor quality rulers may not have correct measurements marked on them. Start with a ruler 3″–6″ wide × 18″–24″ long, and if you continue with quilting, your collection of rulers will grow. Another good purchase is a cork-backed metal ruler designed to stay in place on fabrics, which makes it a consistently accurate measuring tool.

Template Material

You can purchase numerous precut and presized plastic templates for marking quilting patterns, but if you wish to create your own patterns, you will need to purchase special template plastic. Template plastic is a translucent or clear plastic, with one side shiny and the other with a matte finish. Often this plastic has printed grid lines, which helps in placing the pattern on fabrics. If template plastic is not available, used X-ray film works as well. The pattern you desire can be drawn onto the plastic with an extra-fine permanent marker and then cut with a paper scissors or a utility knife.

The same plastics used for the quilting templates can also be used for the templates needed for piecing the quilt top. If you plan to use these templates for other projects, it would be a wise investment in time to cut them out of template plastic. Piece templates should have the seam allowance, usually ¼″, included on the template with the stitching line marked on them for reference. A strip of cellophane, or any clear tape, applied over the stitching line on the template will prevent any ink from transferring to your fabrics.

Heavy paper, preferably with one side coated, is useful for appliqué or one-of-a-kind pieces to be cut. These templates are not as permanent as plastic, but the heavier the paper the longer they can be used. Although standard cardboard is too thick, poster board or oak tag board, available at art supply and craft stores, works beautifully for this type of template. As with the plastic templates, seam allowances should be included and stitching lines marked for reference. Seam allowances are not necessary on appliqué templates, but you may want to use your template as a pressing guide. Just add ¼″ around the piece as you cut it out.

Fabric Marking Utensils

An assortment of marking pens and tools can be used in quilting. The most common is the basic graphite pencil. Graphite pencils, in 2H, HB, or whatever hardness you prefer, don't provide enough contrast on most fabrics to be used for marking quilt patterns (except on very light fabrics) but work perfectly for marking the piece patterns on the reverse side of fabrics for cutting. The pencils need to be as sharp as possible to provide an accurate cutting mark. A recommended alternative to a regular pencil is a 0.5mm technical pencil, which will provide a consistently sharp point; pencil leads can inexpensively be purchased in the softness or hardness desired.

Fabric markers, blue washout markers in particular, are useful and bold enough to use for marking quilt patterns. These markers should be used with extreme care and as sparingly as possible. Before marking any quilt top with a washout marker, test the marker on fabric strips or pieces. The test should include any ironing, pressing, or laundering the quilt will receive. If the marks disappear and cause no problems such as discoloration, the washout marker can be used on

your quilt top. During the process of quilting, the marked fabrics should be kept away from strong light or heat, which could cause the chemical in the markers to react and permanently stain the quilt-top fabrics.

Other useful items that can be used to mark quilting patterns on the quilt tops include small slivers of soap, masking and cellophane tapes, and colored pencils.

Soap remnants, especially thin ones, are great for marking patterns on dark fabrics and will wash out of most fabrics easily. Marks from soap are not permanent and will brush or rub off when handled, and so are best used with simple patterns.

Masking and cellophane tapes are excellent to mark straight runs of quilting on fabrics. The cellophane tape is best for use on satin or silk fabrics and other "glamour"

fabrics. Masking tape can be used successfully on most other quilting fabrics. The tape can be used, lifted, and repositioned several times before replacing, which makes it an economical marking tool. Caution needs to be taken when using any tape for marking fabrics. The quilt top should not be left in sunlight or near heat while using masking or cellophane tapes. The residues in the tape's adhesive may adhere to the fabric and bond with the fibers, which could create a stain that is unremovable. If used for a session of quilting, and then removed at the end of that session, adhesive tapes will provide a quick, easy, and economical device for marking quilt patterns.

Colored pencils, used in drawings or renderings are terrific for marking quilt lines, especially if matched as closely as possible to

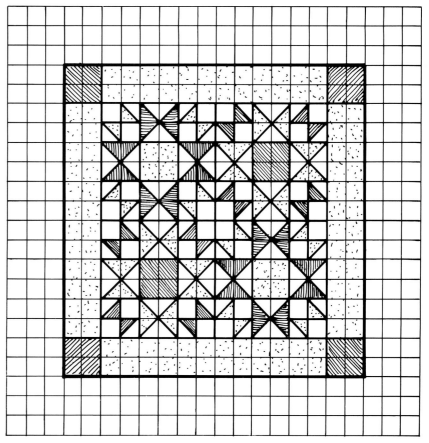

Fig. 3-3. A quilt design created on a grid.

the thread to be used to quilt the pattern. These pencils are of a chalkier substance than regular graphite and can be brushed off the fabric if not applied too heavily.

Design Materials

A very useful tool for marking quilt patterns and in creating templates is the bow compass. The compass is helpful in creating accurate circles and curves of all sizes.

Various types and weights of papers are also useful in quilt projects, most specifically in the design work that needs to be done before any fabrics are cut and sewn together. Grid paper, preferably ¼" scale size, is especially helpful in the initial planning of your quilt top. The grid can be used at full scale (¼" equals ¼") or at half scale (¼" equals ½") for block planning, and even at quarter scale (¼" equals 1") for planning the entire quilt top.

Tracing paper, also known as tracing velum, is also used as a planning tool. The tracing paper can be laid over the drawing you made on the grid paper and value or color tests can be applied. The exact placement of colors and patterned fabrics can be determined and a final version of the sketch used as a piecing guide. The color sketch, in combination with the scaled drawing, can be used for estimating the yardage of fabric you will need to purchase for your quilt project.

Your Work Area

The work surface you use to lay out and cut the pieces of your quilt is also important. Not many of us have a spacious sewing studio with a large table dedicated specifically to the laying out and cutting of fabric. Most people have to improvise on the kitchen or dining

Fig. 3-4. A folding cutting table, like this, is convenient when cutting out your quilt.

room table. Cutting boards for use on tables or even on beds are available for purchase at most fabric stores. The boards are made of heavy-duty cardboard with printed grid and diagonal lines to aid in cutting fabric. The convenience of these boards is that they can be folded and stored. Also, the top surface allows for quilt blocks or pieces to be pinned for more accurate positioning.

Some fabric stores and mail-order catalogs offer a folding cutting/layout table on wheels. The table is at counter height, approximately 36" from the floor, and has two drop leaves that when folded down can be rolled to fit in a space less than 2' wide. As owners of such a table, we can highly recommend this purchase, which provides a sturdy and well-sized surface for cutting and laying out fabrics. Used in combination with a self-healing cutting mat, rotary and regular cutting are made much simpler.

Irons and Ironing Boards

Pressing the seams properly is a critical element in piecing a quilt, and a good iron, whether steam or

dry, is indispensable. The iron you purchase will need to be kept clean and the iron plate free of nicks and residues. Tap water works well for creating steam, but distilled water, which is free of minerals and dissolved chemicals, is even better. The plate on your iron can be cleaned with a piece of terry cloth and water. Many irons now have a built-in cleaning cycle that can help keep the steam holes free of residues from water, dirt, or starch buildup.

A good ironing board is also valuable. The best models have mechanisms to adjust the height, but even a small model placed on a table will work for quilting. The actual ironing surface of the board will need to have a cover and the best ones will have adequate padding and will fit snugly. The materials that ironing board covers are made of varies. Some are heat-resistant, which can protect the surface and board from the heat of the iron. However, this type of cover has a tendency to let water accumulate on the surface of the board, which can cause problems during ironing. A useful ironing board surface for quilting is one of plain muslin. The muslin will not change the fabric colors when heat or moisture is applied. With the addition of a pad and a snug fit, a muslin cover will work well for your quilting needs.

The extent to which you use spray starch in quilting is one of personal preference; the form you use is also up to you. Premixed starch in aerosol cans or in spray bottles work equally well. Although time-consuming, the least expensive starch is the kind you mix yourself. Mixing your own starch can be messy, but with the use of a good sprayer, it can be worth the effort. A good quality plant mister works well as a starch bottle. When mixing your own spray starch, remember to always use warm water. If your pump sprayer or aerosol can clogs, apply warm water to unclog the opening and return the bottle or can to working order.

Pins

To fasten your small and large quilting pieces together, the correct pins are essential. In most cases, when you machine (or hand) stitch a quilt top together, you will not remove the pins as you stitch, so the finest silk pins you can buy will prove to be best for you and your machine. Discard any pins that become dull, nicked, or bent. Any time you sew over a pin with your sewing machine you run the risk of its breaking and lodging in your machine's mechanisms. To alleviate this problem, pull out the straight pins as you come to them while you are sewing.

The best pins for fastening and securing together the layers of a quilt, which can get fairly bulky, are quilter's pins. These pins are longer and heavier than a silk pin and have a larger head. Quilting pins help keep the different layers of a quilt secure for basting. They are also used for pinning a quilt in a quilt frame as well.

If you intend to machine quilt, use safety pins to baste the layers together for stitching. A safety pin can also be used to fasten a group of pieces for a block together for storage and will keep the individual pieces from separating. Purchase the best pins you can, and if cared for and kept from extreme moisture, nickel-plated pins will serve your quilting needs.

Batting

Another important material to consider for your quilt project is the batting layer. The batting is what gives a quilt warmth and surface relief or dimension. Batting comes in many types, thicknesses, and sizes. All have virtues in a quilt. Remember, the thicker the batting, the warmer the quilt. Also, thicker batting makes hand or machine quilting more difficult.

Quilt batting can be made of wool, cotton, or polyester. Wool batting is rarely used today and is difficult, if not impossible, to find. Many antique quilts have wool batting.

Cotton batting is also a traditional batting fiber and is still used by many quilters today for a more traditional look and feel to the finished quilt. It works well for machine quilting because cotton batting slips less than polyester batting, so the quilt layers stay together better. Cotton batting is usually much thinner, has a lower loft, and is easy for the beginning quilter to stitch through.

Cotton batting, if not surface finished, will have a tendency to pull apart into thick and thin areas. This tendency is the reason that quilts with cotton batting need closer quilting than those with a polyester batting of equal loft. If using cotton batting, the quilting lines should be no more than ½" apart.

Several manufacturers have combined pure cotton batting with a thin core of polyester batting to create a thin, stable cotton batting with the nonbunching qualities of polyester.

The newest and most common quilt batting is polyester batting. Most polyester battings have a treated or bonded finish for ease of handling and to keep the fibers from separating when the quilt is laundered, thus keeping the batting from bunching. Polyester battings come in several lofts, ranging from ½" or ¼" to 3" in thickness. The highest loft batting is used primarily for tied quilts and gives a comforter look to a quilt. The most commonly used polyester batting is medium-loft bonded batting with a thickness of ½" to ¾". Intricate hand quilting or quilted clothing requires a low-loft batting ¼" or ½" thick.

The advent of polyester batting dramatically changed the quilting world by making batting more affordable and more stable than the earlier types. Polyester has its shortcomings—it dulls quilting needles and, if used with a fabric containing polyester, can cut the quilting threads. For the most part, however, polyester is the most commonly used quilt batting on the market today.

Needles for Machine and Hand Quilting

For hand quilting, you must purchase needles of sufficient size and quality. Again, as in machine sewing, different needles are suggested for different tasks. For hand sewing, like appliqué or hand piecing, needles called sharps in various sizes are recommended. These needles are long and have highly pointed ends. To quilt, needles called betweens are the best, with the typical sizes being 8, 9, and 10 (the higher the number the smaller the needle). Advanced quilters will use a #12 betweens needle, which is extremely short and thin and, without practice, is difficult to handle. Any betweens needle takes a little practice to use because they are considerably shorter and thinner than a normal needle. Once mastered they are perfect for creating small, even quilt stitches. Experiment with different needles until you find your favorite.

Thimbles

When you purchase your needles, buy a thimble at the same time. Wearing a thimble to quilt is a popular conversation topic with sewers and quilters. To wear or not to wear one is a matter of personal preference. Most quilting and sewing instructions recommend purchasing one and using it, but not everyone can. Also, some people use more than one thimble depending on what they are doing. Thimbles come in all shapes and sizes, from leather ones that nearly cover the entire finger to small metal ones that only cover the tip of your finger. If you have tried a plastic or metal thimble and find that you don't like it because you can't feel where the needle is, a leather thimble is probably better for you. Again, experiment with several types until you find one that works for you — it will definitely save wear and tear on your fingers.

Thread

The thread you choose to work with is also one of personal preference. Although cotton-wrapped polyester thread is acceptable, the best choice is 100% cot-

The many Concord Fabrics materials used in this Log Cabin quilt give it a scrap-quilt look. Quilt by Ann Boyce. Courtesy of Concord Fabrics, New York.

ton thread, for ease of use and the unmistakable look of the natural fiber it produces. Used in combination with all-cotton fabrics, the strength, color, and look are beautiful and impressive. Cotton thread is more expensive but worth it. Check to see what's available in quilting threads at your local fabric or quilting store.

Regular sewing thread can be used for piecing the quilt top, but the recommended thread for the actual hand quilting is specifically called quilting thread. Quilting thread is in the middleweight size between regular thread and buttonhole thread. The range of colors for quilting thread is expanding, which

can create some exciting possibilities. If you choose not to use quilting thread, a double strand of regular sewing thread works as well.

For machine quilting there are also choices in thread. Two basic types are available: nylon "invisible" thread and machine-embroidery thread. Invisible thread is virtually invisible and comes in clear or smoke-colored for use on all fabrics. The nylon is very strong, and if strength is a consideration, this thread is a strong as you can get. The drawbacks of nylon invisible thread is that it can cut certain fabrics, especially fine cottons, and it is hard to knot securely. Also, because the thread is made of plastic, it has a shiny quality that sparkles and shows up in certain lighting situations. Machine-embroidery thread is usually cotton or cotton-wrapped and the effect and strength qualities are very similar to cotton hand-quilting thread.

Fabrics

After collecting the proper equipment, designing the quilt top, and purchasing fabrics, the next step is to prepare your fabrics.

If your quilt will not be used as a table cover, bed cover, or washed in any way, prewashing the fabric is not really necessary. Many quilters prefer the feel, or *hand*, of the fabric directly off the bolt and enjoy piecing and quilting with it. Most quilt projects, though, will require you to test the fabrics for colorfastness and to prewash all the fabrics to minimize shrinkage.

The fabric of choice for most quilters is 100% cotton. All-cotton fabrics drape and sew well, cut beautifully, and have a depth and richness of color and fabric finish that blends and synthetics can't match. They *do* require more care and may cost a little more, but they are definitely worth the money. This is not to say a quilt made of cotton blends or synthetic fibers can't make a beautiful quilt; the choice of fabrics is up to the individual quilter and the effect desired.

"Glamour" fabrics, such as silk, velvet, or satin, are also terrific in quilts. These fabrics are a little harder to work with than cottons but, if handled carefully, can create extremely successful effects. If you intend to use "glamour" fabrics in a quilt, remember not to preshrink as you normally would with cotton fabric. These fabrics must be dry-cleaned, and it is easier (and cheaper) to dry-clean the finished quilt than the many separate pieces of cloth before they are cut and pieced together.

The water temperature preferred for prewashing is warm—not hot or cold—to remove the greatest amount of excess dye and chemicals from the fabrics. The fabrics should be machine washed in gentle dishwashing soap or a soap sold specifically for laundering quilts. Regular laundry detergent is not recommended because it usually contains harsh soaps that can adversely react with the chemicals in new fabrics. However you launder the fabrics at this point is how you should launder the completed quilt in the future.

A test strip or piece should be prepared prior to prewashing for all the fabrics proposed for a quilt. After hand or machine washing, the test pieces should be hand blotted and air dried. If there is no excessive fading or bleeding onto another piece of fabric, you can confidently prewash all the fabrics and machine dry them. If you have problems with one fabric not being colorfast, repeat the process one or

A country look is achieved with Fabric Traditions fabrics and a traditional pattern. Quilt by Jean Wells. Courtesy of Fabric Traditions, New York.

The green Alexander Henry farm print in this quilt gives added interest to this traditional pattern. Quilt by Charlotte Angotti. Courtesy of Alexander Henry Fabrics, Los Angeles.

This quilt, made using V.I.P.'s Remembrance fabrics, gives a Victorian feel with its use of floral prints and muted colors. Quilt by Janet Page. Courtesy of V.I.P. Fabrics, New York.

two times and machine dry the test piece. If the fabric still bleeds onto another color, or continues to fade, scrap that fabric and select an alternate to test and use. This part of the process can be time-consuming and a little tedious, but it is better to spend the time up front instead of washing your finished quilt and getting an unwelcome surprise.

Before applying any markings and cutting any fabrics, press the fabrics as flat as possible. Pressed fabrics are much easier to work with and more accurate to cut from. Lightly starching the fabric pieces makes them much easier to piece together and gives the machine a heftier piece of fabric to "bite" into. This is helpful, especially in sewing tiny pieces together.

Ironing and pressing is important also during the piecing process. *All* seams must be pressed in piecing together a quilt. The general rule of thumb is to press light-colored fabrics over dark-colored fabrics wherever possible. Unlike clothing construction, where seams are pressed open, the small ¼″ quilting seam is pressed to one side to help hold the pieces together and to take some of the stress off the seams.

Cutting

To mark your fabrics for cutting, first lay your fabrics, wrong side up, on your cutting surface. Place a template, right side down, onto your fabric and trace around it with a pencil or marking pen. Be careful to lay the piece on the grain in the direction you want. Continue tracing as many pieces as are required. Share cutting lines when possible. Hand cut the pieces with your dressmaker's shears and stack all the similar pieces together.

If you are using a rotary cutter, place the self-healing plastic cutting matt on your cutting surface. Fold your fabric as much as possible to do multiple cuts of the same piece and then place it on the cutting mat. Arrange the cutting ruler on your folded fabric and begin by trimming approximately ½″ of the side edges to make them even. Remember when using a rotary cutter to always move the knife *away* from you, using an even stroke. When your cut is complete, immediately close the safety shield down on the blade. Again, stack all similar pieces together.

Piecing

To piece the quilt, pin two pieces, right sides together, with straight pins. Be careful not to hit the pins with the sewing-machine needle. Typically, unless otherwise noted, the seam allowance used in quilting is ¼″. Matching squares and rectangles are easy but matching a square and a triangle is more difficult. The best trick to remember is to pin the piece together matching at the seam lines and not the actual edges because oftentimes the pieces will not match up exactly.

The best gauge to use for your sewing machine is in the 10–12 stitches per inch range. This will create a strong seam with few gaps or weak areas.

Appliquéing

In this book the templates for appliqué have been given without seam allowances. You will need to add the ¼″ seam allowance to the pieces while you are cutting them out. In some instances, you may find that you wish to have a larger seam allowance than ¼″.

Draw the pattern for your appliqué on the back side of the fabric with the template face down. Cut around the piece leaving approximately ¼″ seam allowance. After the piece is cut out, fold the seam allowance over the piecing template. You will now use the piecing template as a pressing guide. Press the seam allowance flat with your iron, using starch to stabilize it. You may need to make a few cuts in the seam allowance occasionally to relieve puckers and folds. When you are finished ironing the seam allowance, remove the pressing template. The piece should hold its shape but may need to have another pressing after taking out the template.

At this stage it is ready to be appliquéd to the quilt in its proper position. Blind stitch around the appliqué to secure it to the quilt.

Another way to help stabilize your appliqué is to apply an iron-on interfacing to the back of the appliqué. This will secure the folded-over seam allowance. You will need to cut the interfacing ⅛″ smaller than your template all around.

Quilting

Refer to the Bibliography for specific references on machine piecing, machine quilting, and hand quilting. Machine quilting has become very popular in recent years, and many reference books are available that give excellent instructions on the newest techniques.

You can develop good hand-quilting techniques as you continue to quilt. Most quilters use a running stitch to quilt. In this way, they are able to make a number of stitches at one time. Others use an up-and-down stitching technique, where each stitch is done separately. Depending on which quilting technique you are more comfortable with and which you get used to, you can quilt equally accurate and fast using either.

When you have finished piecing your quilt top and are ready to quilt it, you will need to prepare a backing fabric. On larger quilts this will require you to piece together the backing fabric because most fabrics come in a 44″/45″ or 60″ width. Fabric selection for a 90″ width is very limited.

After you have prepared your backing fabric, lay the piece face down on your work surface. A floor is usually the best place because the fabric needs to lay completely flat and extended. Then put a layer of batting over the piece of backing fabric. Both the backing fabric and batting need to extend at least 12″ around the entire quilt top so that you can affix the quilt in the quilt frame.

Place the quilt top, face up, on top of the other two layers. Make sure that the layers are flat. You will need to pin the three layers together to hold them secure while you baste them. Once you have basted the three layers together you can take out the pins.

If you are hand quilting the quilt, you are now ready to put your quilt into the quilt frame. Depending on the type of quilt frame you have, you can either pin or sew the quilt into the frame. Most frames have some kind of fabric for you to attach the quilt to but there are some that use clamps to hold the quilt in the frame. These do not require you to pin or sew the quilt.

When you have finished quilting, you are ready to take the quilt out of the frame and prepare to bind it. You will need to remove the basting stitches at this stage and

trim away the extra batting and backing fabric so that the edges all align with the quilt edges.

Binding

Bias binding for quilts can be purchased in the notions department of your fabric store, but most quilters prefer to create their own to match or contrast with their quilt top. The binding will finish the edges of the quilt and is relatively easy to make.

First, lay the selected fabric on your work surface wrong side up. Fold one side of the fabric over at a 45-degree angle to determine the bias line. Unfold and mark the bias line. For most quilts a binding 1½″ wide is appropriate. From the initial bias line mark parallel lines that are 1½″ apart. Cut the pieces and match the right sides together for stitching. Stitch together with a ¼″ seam allowance and press it open.

Press one side of the binding under ¼″. It is helpful to use starch to keep the fold in place. To apply the binding to the quilt, lay the quilt "sandwich" face up and flat. Smooth the quilt and place the unfolded edge of the binding to the edge of the quilt with right sides together. Stitch using a ¼″ seam allowance around the entire quilt. When you reach the beginning point, overlap the binding approximately 1½″.

To finish, fold the binding to the back of the quilt. Align the folded edge to the stitching line created when you sewed the binding to the top of the quilt. Hand sew, using a blind stitch, to the backing. Your quilt is now finished.

Other Finishing Techniques

On some quilts or pillows you might want to finish them with a welting. A welting can be created by using a piece of bias fabric pre-

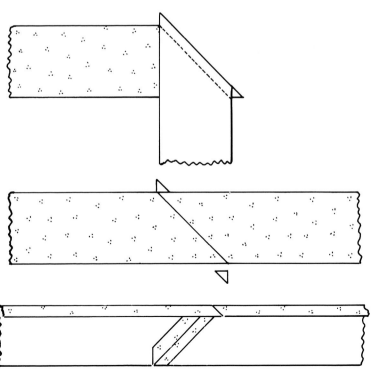

Fig. 3-5. Making bias binding.

This appliqué pillow was done entirely by machine and the edges were finished with prairie points to give a more decorative edge. Pillowcase by Debra Wagner.

pared as the bias binding strips were. A cord of desired size is placed in the middle of the wrong side of the piece and the edges are then folded together. Using a zipper foot on your sewing machine, stitch as close to the cord as possible to create the welting.

There are other finishing methods that can be found in the references listed in the Bibliography. The more you read and learn about quilts the more options you will have to use to embellish them.

Care of Quilts

Above all, the first guideline in caring for quilts, whether they be antique or new, is "easy does it!"

Fabrics, especially old ones, are fragile and are at their most vulnerable when wet or damp.

Laundering

For antique quilts a good airing on a clothesline is the best way to remove dust and any loose soil from the quilt surface. Care must be taken not to hang the quilt in direct sunlight because the sun's rays can further age and weaken old fibers. With an old quilt what you must consider are the consequences if you clean the quilt versus allowing the quilt to remain soiled or stained. Weigh these issues carefully, and if you have any questions, check with a museum curator who deals with antique textiles or a reputable textile dealer.

If you must wash an antique quilt, do so with extreme care. Machine washing is definitely out of the question. Your precious quilt may emerge from the machine in bits. And antique textiles should never be crushed into a small tub. The best place to wash the quilt is in the bathtub or in a child's wading pool if one is available.

Before placing the quilt in the water add a few drops of detergent especially formulated for quilts. Use this gentle soap sparingly; too much soap can be difficult to rinse away. Fold the quilt to fit into the bathtub, with as few folds as possible, and submerge it by hand into lukewarm water. Press the quilt into the water and very gently work it with your hands. Do not wring, scrub too hard or squeeze the quilt — the fibers are at the greatest risk of tearing at this point.

Rinse several times by alternately emptying and filling the tub until all the soap is removed and the water runs clear. Drain the water completely in the last rinse and gently press as much water as possible from the quilt before lifting it out of the tub. Place the quilt flat on clean towels spread over a plastic sheet and let air dry naturally.

Dry-cleaning an antique quilt is an option but is not recommended because the solvents used in the cleaning process can damage and weaken the fibers. Check with a reputable cleaner before attempting to dry-clean an old quilt. If the cleaner hesitates, pursue other cleaning methods.

New quilts, which are made from new fabrics and polyester or bonded cotton batting, can be successfully machine washed. Ideally, however, these quilts should be laundered in the same manner as an antique quilt. Because the majority of new quilts are purchased for use versus display, this method of cleaning may not be an option and instead you will have to machine wash the quilt.

Use warm water, a soap especially formulated for quilts, and the gentle cycle on the washing machine. Carefully remove the quilt from the machine. As with antique textiles, new fabrics are at their most vulnerable when wet. The weight of the wet fabrics can tear the stitching and seams. If possible air dry the quilt using the same method as for antique quilts. If using a clothes dryer to dry your quilt, carefully load the damp quilt into the dryer and dry on the coolest setting. Remove the quilt immediately when dry and lay flat for awhile before storing or rehanging.

Storing

To store quilts, either antique or new, the optimum location is on a bed. This is because the largest portion of the quilt will be flat, ventilation will be best, and the quilt will have minimal contact with wood, plastic, or paper. If you have a sizeable inventory of quilts, however, another method of storage will be necessary.

The three worst enemies to a quilt are moisture or dampness, light, and dirt. Protection from these should be provided for in whatever method of storage you use for your quilt.

Of the three, moisture or dampness is the most damaging to quilts, as well as anything else made of fabric. Quilts should be kept away from extreme humidity, which in some areas can be difficult. Dampness can get into the fibers of your quilt and cause mold and mildew to form, which will ultimately rot the fabrics. Mildew stains are impossible to get out of fabric, so be extremely careful. If stored or displayed in an amply ventilated room with even humidity levels, it is highly unlikely you will have mildew or mold problems.

Exposure to direct sunlight or bright electric light can also cause problems for a quilt. Light will quickly destroy an antique quilt. Even though it may take longer, a new quilt can also suffer from too much exposure to light. If you have ever taken down an old pair of tattered draperies, especially from a room that has been closed for a long time, you have seen the damaging effects of prolonged exposure to light. The same can happen to your treasured quilt.

Dirt and dust can be damaging to quilt fabrics. Excessive dirt can wedge into the quilt fibers and cut or weaken them. The sooner excess dirt and dust can be removed from a quilt the better. Dirt can be a breeding ground for organisms that will eat away the fibers in a quilt.

Quilts are often starched during the construction process, especially those with appliqué. It is not recommended to store quilts for long periods of time with starch remaining on them. Starch is a natural food for small bugs. Storing a quilt with mothballs to repel pests is also not recommended because of the chemicals they contain. Direct contact with the cedar in a cedar chest can also cause problems because of the finish used on the wood. Many herbal and natural pest repellents are available, and your local herb shop can assist you in obtaining the type needed and how best to use them in storing your quilts.

An inexpensive and safe way to store a quilt is to carefully roll or fold the quilt and place it inside an old, washed pillowcase. *Never* store a quilt — or any fabric — in a plastic bag! Plastic bags prevent air from circulating and any moisture in the quilt or bag will not evaporate. The quilt will slowly begin to rot away.

Storing quilts directly against wood, regular boxes, or paper is not recommended because of the damaging acids and chemicals contained in the paper and wood finishes. Acid-free paper and boxes are available and should be used to store fabrics, cut but unpieced quilt tops, pieced quilt tops, and finished quilts. Your local fabric store or wherever you buy your quilt supplies can help you locate acid-free papers and boxes.

When folding a quilt for storage, remember to fold it as few times as possible, as folds will be stress points on the quilt and wear will happen first on these edges. Begin by laying the quilt face up, placing one layer of acid-free tissue paper on the entire top. Next, fold the quilt into thirds and repeat by folding the quilt into thirds again. A single layer of acid-free paper can be placed on the top of each folded area before folding again. It is also recommended to place a roll of acid-free tissue paper on each fold line to prevent sharp creases. Then place the folded quilt into a washed pillowcase, wrap it with an old bed sheet, or wrap it in clean unbleached muslin. Place the quilt into an acid-free box or store on a shelf lined with acid-free paper. This method of storage will work with any thickness of quilt, from a thin coverlet to a superthick quilted comforter.

Another widely accepted method of quilt storage is to roll the quilt. This works best with a thin quilt with minimal bulk. A large plastic or cardboard tube, at least 5″ in diameter and covered in acid-free paper or washed unbleached muslin, will work well. Roll the quilt onto the tube, again placing acid-free tissue paper on the top. The rolled tube can be stored on brackets or on a shelf lined with acid-free paper.

No matter how you store your quilts, remove them from their storage boxes or rolls and unfold them at least every six months. When refolding them use new, clean, acid-free paper and change the location of the folds to prevent excess wear on the earlier folds. If possible, place the quilts flat for a week or so to air them and to rest the fabric fibers. Not only is removing quilts from storage on a regular basis good for them, but it also give you an opportunity to look at them and consider rotating them in and out of storage.

Hanging and Exhibiting

Quilts are typically displayed on beds, but as this book shows there are many other places to display your quilts. If you wish to display an antique quilt, it is best to speak with an expert before doing anything that might harm the quilt.

An antique quilt, or one showing any wear or disintegration of the quilt fabrics, should not be on a bed. Consider having the quilt mounted on a piece of acid-free mounting board and placed in a Plexiglas, box-type frame for protection. A professional frame shop or art gallery can direct you if you wish to pursue this display idea. When positioning the display box, avoid high light level areas or spots with direct sunlight and heat.

The most popular and common method used to hang a quilt is to use a rod pocket and wall-mounted quilt rod. This works best for new quilts and for older quilts in good condition. An extremely heavy quilt is not a good candidate for hanging with a rod pocket. The added stress on the edge of the quilt will cause it to sag and stretch. It could also tear the quilt fabrics. A rod pocket can be created from a piece of backing fabric on a new quilt or of washed and pressed unbleached muslin on an old quilt.

To create a rod pocket for a quilt, first place the quilt face down and smooth flat. Measure the width of the quilt edge that is to receive the rod pocket and cut a piece of fabric 6″ wide and 2″ longer than the hanging edge of the quilt. Next fold and press under ½″ on each end of the strip and fold under again 1″. Hand stitch with a blind stitch or machine stitch and press flat. Fold the entire strip lengthwise with wrong sides together and stitch on the long edge using a ⅝″

seam allowance. Press the seam open. Press the entire rod pocket flat, centering the seam down the middle of the rod pocket. Lay the rod pocket on the quilt back, with the seam side down. The rod pocket should be centered at least ½″ down from the sides and top of the quilt. The top edge of the pocket should be as straight as possible. Pin the rod pocket to the quilt and hand sew, using a blind stitch. To hang, slide the hanging rod through the pocket and smooth the quilt along the pocket. Hang on the wall as desired.

> **Note:** Never pin, nail, tack, glue, or otherwise directly fasten a quilt to a wall.

Another method to hang a quilt is to create a muslin strip 2″–3″ wide and 2″ longer than the edge of the quilt. Fold all edges under ½″ and press flat. Cut 6″ strips of Velcro, separate, and machine stitch the long edges of the Velcro loop strip onto the right side of the muslin or backing fabric strip. Space the Velcro strips evenly along the fabric strip before stitching. Center the Velcro/fabric strip on the quilt, similar to how a rod pocket is placed, pin, and hand sew the strip to the quilt back. Using special glue for Velcro, attach the other (hook) side of the Velcro strip to a thin strip of board that is the same width as the quilt. Secure the board to the wall, then press the quilt loop strip onto the hook strip of the Velcro to hang the quilt.

An interesting new way to hang a quilt has appeared recently in mail-order catalogs. A "quilt clamp," which is as long as the quilt is wide, consists of two finished boards that separate so that one edge of the quilt can be clamped between them when the boards are tightened. The quilt can then be hung on the wall where desired (the clamp is placed on nails or pegs) without adding or attaching any fabric to a quilt. The pressure on the hanging edge of the quilt would be even, and the actual quilt surface would not be pierced in any way.

If using this method, we recommend, as with any method, that you remove the quilt regularly so that it can rest for a week or two. Because the clamps cut off air circulation to the fabrics, which are clamped under the boards, you will need to rest the quilt more often than with other methods. It is a good idea to have additional quilts that can replace ones that need to be rested. Seasonal quilts work well to help you remember to rest your quilts—as the season changes so does the quilt.

Quilts can also be hung over chairs, quilt racks, tables, or wherever you wish them to appear. Wherever possible place a piece of clean unbleached muslin between your quilt and any wood to keep the wood finish from staining or ruining the backing fabric. With a little care and consideration, your quilts can be used and still look beautiful for years to come.

Color

Color, and how color is perceived, is a very personal and subjective process. We all see colors in a unique way, and how we feel about certain colors can illicit many individual responses. Each person has an inborn, innate sense of color. Our own color preferences as to what is harmonious or discordant

This quilt rack is on a pivot base so that you can adjust the angle and the distance it sits from the wall. It is a good option for a narrow space.

to each of us are also personalized. How we use that color sense also differs from person to person, with some exhibiting more confidence than others in their color selections.

Color is also a science, or at best covered under several different sciences. Color and the theory of color have been studied for many years by physicists, psychologists, and physicians, as well as artists and scholars.

The more technical aspects of color fall under the realm of physics, which studies the physical properties and composition of color. Physicists study the electromagnetic spectrum, of which the area of visible color is a very small band. The study of the physical properties of color was originated by Sir Isaac Newton, who in the late seventeenth century refracted white light

through a prism, which separated and dispursed it into the spectrum of visible color. Visible color lies between the very short waves of cosmic, gamma, and X-rays and the longer rays of infrared radiation, microwaves, television, and radio waves, and, ultimately, electric power. The human eye can perceive light waves between 360 and 760 nanometers on the electromagnetic spectrum. A nanometer is a metric unit of measure, in which, for example, 30 nanometers measure only 15 billionths of an inch.

An object by nature does not have an actual color; only when light is shown on the object can color be registered. Color is registered when an object reflects that color, such as red on a vase or a fabric, and all the other colors of the spectrum are absorbed.

Color in our world is most often done by dyes and pigments, an absorptive process, and the colors produced follow the rule of subtraction. To briefly explain, color produced by combining the primary colors of light differ from the primary colors of pigments. A primary color is one that cannot be created by mixing other colors. The additive primaries of light are cyan (blue-green), magenta (blue-red), and yellow. When combined together, the end result is white. Subtractive primaries, which is where pigments fall, have primary colors of red, yellow, and blue. Combining these three colors will result in a dark gray-black. When pigment colors are mixed, all colors are absorbed, except the color created, which is subtracted and then transmitted by reflection to the eye.

The physiological process of how the eye actually sees color is in reality a chemical process. When light enters the eye, a chemical reaction occurs in three different re-

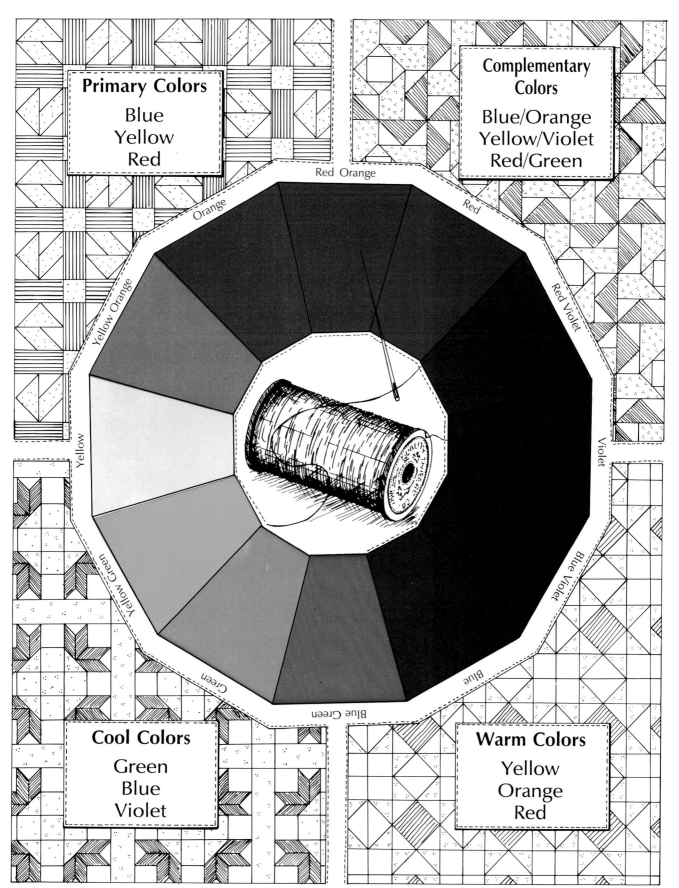

Primary Colors

Blue
Yellow
Red

Complementary Colors

Blue/Orange
Yellow/Violet
Red/Green

Cool Colors

Green
Blue
Violet

Warm Colors

Yellow
Orange
Red

Red Orange
Orange
Yellow Orange
Yellow
Yellow Green
Green
Blue Green
Blue
Blue Violet
Violet
Red Violet
Red

Fig. 3-6. The basics of the color wheel.

The use of pure, bright colors adds a vibrancy to this quilt called *Trip Around the Spectrum*. An occasional black border helps to tone the colors down slightly and gives an interesting variation to a traditional pattern.

ceptors (called cones), in which each type reacts to a different one of the primary colors of light: cyan, magenta, and yellow. In times when light levels are high, the cones are working at their most efficient and we therefore have our best rendition of color. As light levels change, so does the efficiency of the cones in our eyes. Moving from areas of high to low light, blues will be perceived better and sharper than when we move to from low to high light, in which objects in red will be seen clearer. As light levels get lower, the cones cease to work as effectively and do not respond to

color as well. A second type of receptor called a rod comes into play, providing us with low light level vision, but that doesn't provide color perception. This explains why colors are so much more difficult to see at night.

Systems have been developed to further define and name colors, the most recognized being the Ostwald and Munsell systems. Both systems have different approaches to naming colors. The Ostwald system uses a code to define shades, tints, and tones of colors, whereas the Munsell system deals most with hue, value, and chroma.

For our use in quilting, we will base our colors on those created from pigments and a simple color wheel. The three primary colors of red, blue, and yellow combine to create the secondary colors of orange, green, and purple. Combinations of these primary and secondary colors result in myriad other colors, but all are variations on these six colors.

Colors directly opposite on the color wheel are called complementary colors. To make a color grayer, add a little of the complementary color. The resulting grayed color will be much more harmoni-

CHAPTER FOUR

Quilts All Through the House

The next two chapters are devoted to giving you ideas for using quilts in ways that you may not have thought of otherwise.

Any room in your home is a perfect spot for some kind of quilt, whether it be a quilted shower curtain in a bathroom or a quilted runner on a coffee table. Many people think of quilts as being only on beds, but for someone who appreciates quilts, the sky's the limit.

Quilts work especially well in areas such as a stairway landing or an entryway where a large, decorative piece is called for. A quilt can also be draped over a balcony railing, if you have a home with vaulted ceilings, which opens the second floor area into the rest of the living space.

The photographs that follow show just a sampling of the possibilities for decorating your home in quilts.

This quilt adds a nice touch to a railing overlooking the first floor family room. It decorates both the family room and the upstairs loft.

Entryway, Hallways and Stairways

Set the tone of your home with a quilt in the entrance to welcome guests. It can either be a quilt over a table or a quilted art piece on the wall.

Decorating with quilts doesn't automatically mean you have to use only quilts. There are many other decorative items that incorporate a quilt motif. Many of these are designed with a country flair, but in the right setting they work equally well for a contemporary home. There are now rugs that incorporate traditional quilt patterns in their designs that could give your entryway an inviting look.

A transfer medium was used to print Xerox copies of Charlie Chaplin onto fabric, creating this unique wall hanging. After the piece was quilted, it was stretched over canvas stretchers. This particular quilt was not framed, though it could be.

This quilt uses Call of the Wild fabrics in its design, and the hallway works well to display it. Quilt by Janet Page. Courtesy of V.I.P. Fabrics, New York.

Two quilts were stacked to help fill this large area in a stairwell. Note that these two quilts are made from the same pattern. This is an excellent example of how different a quilt can look by changing the colors and the fabrics.

Stairway landings are an excellent place to show off quilts. One large quilt can be displayed in this space or a grouping of smaller quilts can be arranged to fill the area.

Hallways can be used as a quilt gallery with your newest quilted art on display until the next quilt is ready for its unveiling. Another idea is to have seasonal quilts and to change them throughout the year because your quilts will last longer if you rest them occasionally.

Living Room and Family Room

The living room and family room offer many possibilities for decorating with quilts. In the winter, throw a quilt across your sofa or favorite chair. This will add interest to your room as well as serve the utilitarian purpose of keeping you warm.

Other possibilities include table covers on coffee tables or end tables. In the projects section, see the Game Board pattern. This pattern works well in a family room because you can use it as a table square for a favorite decorative piece until you're ready to play checkers.

The Rail Fence pattern works well for this throw, which can be displayed over the back of the chair when not in use and is convenient when needed.

This family room shows how you can use several quilts in the same room. As long as the colors harmonize you can mix quilts and patterns to come up with your own look. Quilt on sofa pieced by Blanche Johnson, quilted by the author.

The table square on the coffee table converts to a game board when you are ready for a game of checkers.

Don't be afraid to mix patterned fabrics when creating quilted wall hangings to go with your home. Here a dogwood quilt block with floral border combines effectively with the French country look of the sofa. Courtesy of Mary Ciurlino.

This wall quilt decorates a passthrough into another room. Quilt by Ann Boyce. Courtesy of Concord Fabrics, New York.

Quilts can be used to decorate coffee tables in more formal settings, as shown here. Quilt by Ann Boyce. Courtesy of Fabric Traditions, New York.

Wall quilts can be used in these rooms, too. You would probably choose a less formal wall quilt for your family room than you would for your living room.

If you have shelves in these rooms you might decide to make a shelf liner. The shelf liner can be strictly decorative or it can be used to hide items such as VCRs or in an entertainment center if two shelves are close enough together. The pattern for a shelf liner in the projects section was designed to cover up the VCR and shelf in an armoire.

If you are making strictly decorative shelf liners chances are you will want a shorter drop on the front, which will mean a simpler design pattern. The fabrics you choose for your shelf liner will depend on what you plan to set on it. Washable fabrics are best because they can be laundered as they get soiled by everyday dust. "Glamour" fabrics should be used for more seasonable projects that will only be out a short while.

Another way to bring quilts into your living room and family room is with the use of pillows. Make either small throw pillows using your favorite block pattern or larger floor pillows. A good size for a floor pillow to sit on is approximately 30″. Usually, the largest pillow form you can find is 20″, so use the 20″ form and wrap it in batting to make your 30″ pillow form. Floor pillows work well for casual decorating, and children love them.

Traditional Amish quilt patterns were adapted to make a wall quilt and two 30″ floor pillows for this home.

Dining Room

Quilts in the dining room can add a very distinctive look to your home. Once again wall quilts can be used if there is an appropriate location in the room.

There are many options open to you for using quilts on the dining table, such as a single table runner, multiple table runners, placemats, or a quilt that covers the entire table top. You can also use quilts in conjunction with tablecloths to give a layered look.

When deciding on a treatment to be used, take into account the style and look you desire. Although, placemats usually suggest a more informal setting, you can make some elegant placemats with "glamour" fabrics such as taffeta, satin, and brocade.

Table runners can take many forms. A single, narrow runner in the middle of the table works with an oblong or rectangular table and a round runner fits a round table. Multiple runners, laid across a rectangular table, can also work as placemats. A table runner can be a nice accent to your dining table during the times between meals when you would like to show off the look of the table itself.

Tablecloth quilts work well to protect tables from scratches and moisture due to normal use. The fabrics used to construct these quilts should be washable. Cotton fabrics or cotton blends work the best. The quilts will also help protect the table surfaces from damage due to heat from hot dishes, although trivets should still be used for very hot dishes taken directly from oven to table.

The *Patriotic Placemats* pattern was designed to create placemats for a more relaxed table setting.

Whatever your decorating style, you can create a quilt to fit. Here a tropical quilted wall hanging brings color to a dining room. Quilt made by Janet Page from Rainforest fabrics. Courtesy of V.I.P. Fabrics, New York.

Frank Lloyd Wright's designs were the inspiration for this long, narrow table runner, which was updated with contemporary colors and fabrics.

Three runners in the same style and colors give the table a different look.

The quilted table cover works well with the contemporary furniture and helps soften the look of the room. Quilt by Ann Boyce. Fabric by Timeless Treasures, Hi-Fashion Fabrics, Inc., New York.

A Crazy Quilt pattern was used to create chair cushions and a matching table cover in this dining room set. The decorative stitching on the quilt was done by machine.

This quilt works as a tablecloth and gives the table setting a country feel. Quilt by Debra Wagner.

Here a table runner combined with a tablecloth gives a formal look. Notice how the leaves in the table runner break out of the rest of the rectangle. Irregular shapes can add interest to your quilts.

Quilts used with tablecloths can provide an elegant, Victorian look or a warm country feel, depending on the quilts and tablecloths used. Experiment with different combinations to come up with a look suitable to your taste.

Quilts can also be used on accessory pieces of furniture in the dining room, such as a sideboard. Make a table runner, shelf liners, or small quilts to use as doilies under decorative pieces placed on a sideboard or hutch unit.

Quilted chair seat covers are another way to bring quilts to your dining room. If you are covering the chair pads with a quilted covering, you will need to consider the seat shape when deciding on what quilt pattern to use. A crazy quilt pattern with decorative machine stitching can work well for odd-shaped chair pads. Depending on your color and fabric choices, you can create a formal or informal look using a crazy quilt pattern.

When deciding on fabrics for chair covers, choose fabrics that will hold up to wear and tear. Once again, cotton fabrics are a good choice. It is best to look for upholstery fabrics versus quilting calicoes when doing quilted treatments for furniture.

Kitchen

Quilts in the kitchen can take many forms. You can make quilted appliance covers, potholders, tea or coffee cozies, or baking and casserole dish covers, to name a few. If you have a table in the kitchen, you

You can create your own quilted cooking accessories. Thicker batting is used to give this casserole cozy and matching potholders more insulation.

can make quilted placemats or a tablecloth, much the same as those described for the dining room (see above). You can also decorate towels with quilted sections.

Quilts in the kitchen are usually smaller and would definitely make good projects for a first-time quilter who would rather make something other than a wall quilt.

Bedrooms

This is the room of the house where most people think of using quilts. Quilts are beautiful additions to a bedroom and can make the bed the central focus of the room. It's also a good place to show off elaborate quilting because of the size the quilts have to be to cover the bed.

You can dramatically change the look of your bedroom by changing the quilts on the bed. It's fun to collect seasonal quilts and to change the bedding throughout the year. This will give the room a fresh, new look with each season, without a major decorative overhaul, and rotating your quilts will help preserve them for a longer period of time.

You can also make quilted dresser scarves and covers for dressing tables and benches to bring a continuity to your bedroom. If you have a cedar chest or blanket chest, a quilt placed over the top of the chest will help protect it from wear or damage.

This quilt shows a variation on the Triple Irish Chain. Elaborate quilting is displayed on the drops on the sides and foot of the bed. Antique pillowcases and pillow sham contribute to the country feel. As an added accent, the cedar chest is covered with a small quilt. Cedar chest quilt by Julie Schlarman.

If you have an appropriate spot, you can have a wall quilt in your kitchen. Quilt by Debra Wagner.

The look of the bed is changed with these commercially made quilts and shams. A colorful Trip Around the World pattern is mixed with a white battenburg lace quilt and pillow sham to give the bed a new look.

Another piece usually, but not always, found in a bedroom is a quilt rack. You can use this to hang your extra quilts. You may also want to combine other textiles with your quilts on the rack. Heirloom pieces such as pillowcases with crocheted lace edges or vintage embroidery patterns look lovely combined with your favorite quilts. These pillowcases can also be used on the bed in combination with quilted throw pillows and pillow shams to give a very comfortable, overstuffed, nostalgic look to your bedroom.

Mix patterns together to give your room individuality. Any combination will work as long as you like the result, but as a rule of thumb, you are usually safe if you work within the same color combinations. Trial and error is the best way to create a room that is uniquely yours.

A contemporary wall quilt in mixed fabrics, including a peach satin, works in this bedroom with an antique bed quilt. Wall quilt courtesy of Chilton Book Company; bed quilt by Nellie Moyle.

Children's Rooms

Quilts for children can be the most fun to make of all the quilts created for a home. Imagination is the key.

Baby quilts can be very rewarding to make. You can make quilts with pastels and cute animals or bright colors and geometric patterns. A one-of-a-kind pictorial quilt can be used to decorate a nursery wall, and one that the child can eventually pass on to his or her own children.

In this sampler baby quilt a bunny tries to climb through the blocks and lattice. The ears flop on the ends and the bunny has been done in trapunto to give it a three-dimensional look. Courtesy of Kelley Moore.

The quilt on the crib is commercially made. Matching fabrics were purchased to create the trapunto wall quilt, teddy bear, and pillow. Courtesy of Joseph Ciurlino.

From the baby quilt you can take a part of the pattern to create other accessory pieces. Some possibilities include pillows, dolls, teddy bears, diaper bags, and bumper pads. Some of these pieces can be used as the child gets older if they are designed for children and not just infants. Keep this in mind as you choose a pattern and color combination for your nursery.

As children get older and change from cribs to beds, you can make bed-size quilts to replace the crib quilt. You can also make quilted wall hangings to decorate their walls.

In the projects section, see the Pencil Wall Quilt. This project can be adapted to work with any color combination and the irregular shape makes it a unique piece. Also see the Naptime Clown Quilt and Pillow, a motif that can help to make naptime a little more fun for a toddler.

It can be interesting to get your children involved in designing and making their own quilts. They may come up with suggestions that will make the quilt truly their own. Until they are old enough to hand quilt with a needle or work with a sewing machine, tied quilts are a good way to get young children started in quilting.

The Sunbonnet Sue motif in the quilt was also used to make a rectangular pillow and a Sunbonnet Sue doll. Courtesy of Emily Moore.

Bathrooms

Because typically a bathroom is not very large, it does not allow for a lot of quilting possibilities. However, one idea for a quilt in your bathroom is a quilted shower curtain, which can be a striking addition and a conversation piece. When making and using a quilt for a shower curtain, use flannel in place of batting to keep the weight and thickness of the quilt to a minimum, and a plastic shower liner to keep most of the water off the quilt, as well as off the floor.

If you have the space, you can also make a wall quilt for the bathroom. Wall quilts can be as small as you need them to be. You can create a single square of your favorite traditional quilt block, stretch it over canvas stretchers, and frame it to hang in a small area where there is not enough room for a larger quilt.

Towels can be decorated with quilted sections to bring continuity to your bathroom. You may also want to accessorize with items that have a quilt motif. Look for terry cloth towels in traditional quilt pattern prints that have matching rugs to coordinate with them. If you use your imagination, you can decorate your bathroom from top to bottom in quilts.

The *Patriotic Placemats* bring a festive touch to your summer picnics.

The leaves on this autumn quilt were stencilled rather than appliquéd. Stencilling allows for a little more delicate detail than appliquéing.

Seasonal Quilts

The possibilities are nearly limitless when it comes to seasonal quilts. You can either decorate with holiday-specific quilts or general seasonal quilts.

You may be able to find a wall in your home where you can hang quilts and change them throughout the year as holidays come and go. Or you may wish to make quilted table covers that can be used for each new season.

The Patriotic Placemats in the projects section, celebrating Memorial Day, the Fourth of July, and Labor Day, can be used throughout the summer.

A quilt in browns, golds, and oranges can make an attractive fall quilt, which can be used from late September to the Thanksgiving holiday.

December offers myriad choices for quilted projects. You can quilt decorative pieces to celebrate either Channukah or Christmas. Then create a festive quilt to ring in the New Year in style!

Through January and February, you can display quilts with a winter motif or ones that are holiday-specific, such as quilts for Valentine's Day or President's Day.

March brings in St. Patrick's Day with its traditional greens and clovers. It also starts off the first thoughts of spring, so a quilt with a floral motif would be appropriate.

Whatever your seasonal preferences, you can set the mood you wish to convey with quilts.

This welcoming holiday wreath was decorated in quilted stars.

Stockings can be created in many styles to match your decorating taste. Here stencilling was used to help decorate some of the fabric. Houses courtesy of Dina Mancini.

The tree is decked out in quilted ornaments that were stencilled. Matching fabrics were used to create the tree skirt, which is a variation of the pattern in the projects section. The window is decorated with Christmas balls and quilted stars to carry out the decorating theme. House decorations on the tree courtesy of Dina Mancini.

An elegant look was brought to this Christmas display by the use of taffeta, satin, and lamé fabrics.

This shelf liner was created with satin to give the look of snow when the Christmas village is set up on it.

The Tree of Life quilt pattern was stencilled on this Christmas throw. Not only is it a nice addition to your holiday decorating, but the throw can be handy on cold nights. Quilt by Lynn Gianiny.

CHAPTER FIVE

Designing a Quilt to Fit Your Needs

Things to Consider

Style

Once you've decided that you want a quilt, the first thing to do is to get an idea of the style and pattern you like. Look through quilting books and flag pages with quilts and color combinations you like. Also, clip pictures from magazines of quilts that catch you eye and keep a file for later reference. Whether you are going to make the quilt yourself or have someone else do it, this file will be useful. The pictures of quilts you flag or clip need not be exactly what you want, as long as they have some aspect you like. It may be a border detail, a medallion, or a color combination. It's difficult for most people to visualize in their head what a quilt will look like, so the use of an idea file helps.

This quilt was designed as a retirement gift for a teacher. The different items on the quilt are reminders of her class. The center tablet sheet lists the names of the family members who were her students and the year she taught them. Courtesy of Pat Taylor.

Size

Your next step is to decide what size quilt you need. If you are doing a wall quilt, make certain that it is in proportion to the space where it is to be displayed. Do not make it fill the entire space. So as not to make it look crowded, leave some space around a wall quilt. Larger quilts should probably be used on a wall by themselves or as a backdrop, whereas smaller quilts can be used on a wall with other decorations or above pieces of furniture.

Table covers can be whatever size you like. Your own personal taste will help you decide what you want. The size can vary depending on if you want a small quilt to act as a table runner or table square or a larger quilt to hang over the table edge. If the quilt is for more decorative purposes than for use as a tablecloth when entertaining, you may want a longer drop. You may also want to place the quilt at a slight angle, or on point, for a more decorative and personal flare. This style can be used in conjunction with tablecloths for a layered look.

Other areas you may wish to decorate, such as with shelf liners, shower curtains, and chair covers, will have very specific dimensions to them. Quilts for beds need to be a certain size also, although the drop on the sides and foot of the quilt can vary depending on the style of bed and the look you want. If you want a coverlet you can use 14″ as a basis for the drop, but if you're looking for a quilted bedspread you will have to measure the distance from the top of your mattress to the floor to figure the drop length. Another thing to take into account when designing a bed quilt is the style of bed. On a four-poster bed you may want to cut out the corners of the drop so that it will lay

This quilt block was made of cotton fabrics and silver lamé. It was then stretched over canvas stretchers, framed, and hung on point. A framed quilt block is a terrific option for small areas.

flat around the posts instead of bunching up.

The next step is to actually design the quilt within the size you need. Refer back to your idea file. Either adapt the pattern from a picture you like, or take aspects of a few quilts and create your own new design. If this is to be your first quilt, start with a simple pattern consisting of squares and triangles, which many traditional patterns are based on, rather than a design with thousands of tiny pieces.

An easy first quilt is one of all squares made from leftover scraps of fabric. Another project to consider is a pattern called Trip Around the World. This pattern is made of rows of squares that form diamonds of color *because* of the placement of blocks. Traditionally this pattern is centered, but see the projects section for a pattern called Off-Center Trip Around the World Quilt. Other beginner's projects are the Game Board or Wild Blue Rose Quilt, also in the projects section. Both are made of triangles and squares and the pieces are a good size to work with.

Color

After you've designed your quilt it is time to think about color. First design the overall look of the quilt by taking a ballpoint pen and filling in a drawing of the quilt with different patterns and values to see how you want the contrast to accentuate your design.

Before you take this drawing to the fabric store, you may want to fill in colors in place of the patterns and values.

Don't be in a rush to make your quilt in the very first color layout you come up with. Play with the design by changing the placement of the colors. You'll be surprised at how different the quilt can look. It's well worth your time and effort to do this now before you've sewn it all together and then decide you don't like it.

Fabric

Be flexible with your color choices once you get to the fabric store. Even if you think you've seen all the fabrics at your local fabric store and know just exactly what you want, they may be out of what you are looking for or they may have new fabrics you haven't seen yet. You may also find a fabric that you can't live without and it may suggest a new color combination. If you're making the quilt to go with other things in the room, bring

The wall quilt and pillows in this room were designed to go with the chair. An arm cover was taken to the fabric store to match colors and fabrics. Courtesy of Rick and Denise Moore.

along a color sample such as a paint chip, a throw pillow, or an arm cover.

Selection of fabric can be a complicated but enjoyable task. Don't rush yourself when making choices. You will have the quilt for a long time and you want it to look right. Not only are you selecting color and patterns, you also need to decide on the type of fabric.

For most projects, and for the first-time quilter, cotton or cotton-blend fabrics work best because they are more stable and tend not to stretch. But eventually you may want to branch out into other types of fabrics. Taffeta, lamé, satin, and brocade can add some interesting

textures and colors to your quilts. Because most of these "glamour" fabrics have to be dry-cleaned, you should use them only for decorative quilts. Check the care instructions on the bolt of fabric to see how to take care of it. For useful books on care and characteristics of fabrics, refer to the Bibliography.

Once you have chosen your fabrics and know better how the fabrics look together, do another color rendering of the quilt in case you want to do some adjusting. If you stay flexible during this whole process, you can end up with a better-looking, more interesting quilt.

Now you're ready to cut out, piece, and quilt or tie your quilt (see Chapter Three, Quilting Basics). Here again, there is no reason to rush. Take your time and do it right and you will have a quilt to enjoy for a long time.

Buying Quilts

With the new interest in quilts, many department stores and mail-order catalogs now offer hand-quilted quilts at good prices. Many of these are made in China and imported into the United States. As with anything, you get what you pay for. Experience has shown that these quilts do not have the quality of the good hand quilting done by many quilters. However, if this is all you can afford, then this is a way to bring quilts into your home.

Another option is to attend crafts shows and fairs in search of a quilt, or quilts, to fit your needs. This allows you to check out the quality of the quilt in person, but you may have to settle for whatever color combinations are available.

If you want a custom-made quilt, you will need to find a quilter to work with you. Many of the quilters at crafts fairs will be glad to make quilts on request and to specification. Another place to check is at your local fabric or quilting store. If they are a customer-oriented store, they will know the names of some quilters who frequent their shop and who may be willing to make you a quilt.

PART III

Quilt Projects

CHAPTER SIX

Practical Quilts

Patriotic Placemats

(Finished dimensions: 12½″ × 17½″ for each placemat.)

These placemats were designed for summer gatherings, but the simple design can be adapted to any color combination and dressed up with fancier "glamour" fabrics. Another advantage to the simplicity of these patterns is that you can show off your quilting skills by elaborately quilting a decorative pattern. The size and pattern also allows you to try machine quilting if you've never done it before.

Fabric Requirements

Fabric 1: ¼ yard of white-on-white print
Fabric 2: ¼ yard of red print
Fabric 3: ¼ yard of navy blue print
Fabric 4: 2¼ yards of navy blue solid

Quantities Needed

Note: This project does not require using templates; all fabrics can be cut as strips. All strip measurements include the standard ¼″ seam allowances.

Placemat A

Fabric 1: cut 2 strips, 3″ × 18″
Fabric 2: cut 2 strips, 3″ × 18″
Fabric 3: cut 1 strip, 3″ × 18″

Placemat B

Fabric 1: cut 2 strips, 4″ × 13″
Fabric 2: cut 2 strips, 4″ × 13″
Fabric 3: cut 1 strip, 4″ × 13″

Placemat C

Fabric 1: cut 4 strips, 3″ × 7½″
Fabric 2: cut 6 strips, 3″ × 7½″
Fabric 3: cut 1 strip, 4″ × 13″

Placemat D

Fabric 1: cut 2 strips, 3″ × 4″; cut 2 strips, 3″ × 11″
Fabric 2: cut 3 strips, 3″ × 4″; cut 3 strips, 3″ × 11″
Fabric 3: cut 1 strip, 4″ × 13″

Backing: cut from Fabric 4

Binding: make 2 yards of binding from Fabric 4 for each placemat

1. Prewash and dry the fabrics, then iron flat. If you are using "glamour" fabrics, check the end of the fabric bolt for washing instructions. Cut out the strips of fabric according to the dimensions given above.

2. Placemat A: Piece together the strips with right sides together, on the long edge in the following order: Fabric 2, Fabric 1, Fabric 3, Fabric 1, and Fabric 2. Press all seam allowances in one direction and set aside.

3. Placemat B: Join the fabric strips, with right sides together, on the long edge in the following order: Fabric 2, Fabric 1, Fabric 3, Fabric 1, and Fabric 2. Stitch and press the seam allowances. Set aside.

4. Placemat C: Stitch the 3" × 7½" strips, joining at the long edges, with right sides together, as follows: Fabric 2, Fabric 1, Fabric 2, Fabric 1, and Fabric 2. Press all seam allowances and repeat with remaining 3" × 7½" strips. Join one pieced section to one long edge of the Fabric 3 strip and repeat with the second pieced section on the other long edge. Press the seam allowances and set aside.

5. Placemat D: Use the same process as for Placemat C, with one pieced side utilizing the 3" × 4" strips and the other the 3" × 11" strips. Press the seam allowances and set aside.

6. Quilt and bind as desired. Refer to Chapter Three, Quilting Basics.

You can be creative with your quilting on these placemats. Stars and firecrackers were used to amplify the patriotic theme shown here.

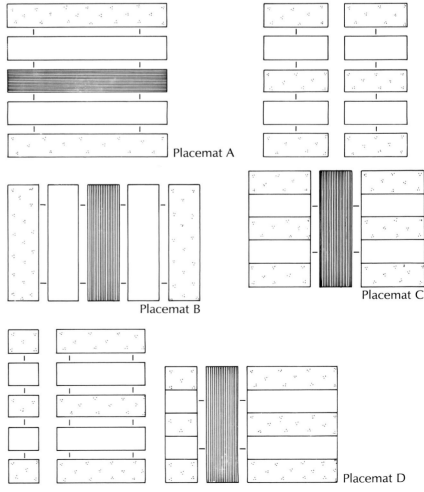

Fig. 6-1. Piecing diagram for the placemats.

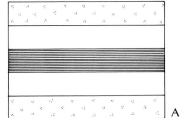
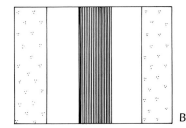
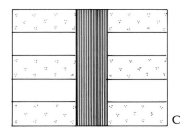

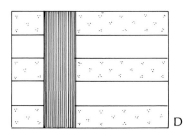

Fig. 6-2. Finished placemats.

Cottage Placemats and Tea Cozy

(Finished dimensions: 10″ × 15″ for each.)

This project will solicit comments at your next afternoon tea. The same pattern works for both the tea cozy and the placemats. We added some hand embroidery to ours to give the impression of vines, but this is not necessary if you wish to have a simpler cottage.

Fabric Requirements

Note: Fabric requirements are for four placemats and one tea cozy. You will actually need to make six placemats as the tea cozy is constructed from two of these. Yardages should be altered if you wish to do a different number of placemats.

Fabric 1: 2 yards of pale pink print
Fabric 2: ¼ yard of forest green print
Fabric 3: ¼ yard of light blue print

Fabric 4: ¼ yard yellow print
Fabric 5: 2 yards of ivory solid

Quantities Needed

Windows: cut 12 of Fabric 4
Window trim: cut 24 of Fabric 3
Doors: cut 6 of Fabric 3
Roof: cut 48 of Fabric 2
Roof peak: cut 24 strips, 1½″ × 6½″, of Fabric 1

Door side of cottage: cut 6 strips, 1½″ × 6½″, of Fabric 1; 60 strips, 1½″ × 2½″, of Fabric 1
Window side of cottage: cut 2 strips, 1½″ × 9½″, of Fabric 1; 24 strips, 1½″ × 2½″, of Fabric 1; 48 strips, 1½″ × 2″ of Fabric 1
Backing: cut from Fabric 5
Binding: cut from Fabric 1

Placemats

Note: Directions are for one placemat. Repeat steps for each additional placemat required.

Embroidery was added to give the look of a vine-covered cottage.

1. Prewash and dry the fabrics, then iron flat. Place the templates on each color of fabric, mark patterns, and cut out. Also cut out all the strips required for this project.

2. Pin together roof strips with eight strips per section of roof. Stitch together using ¼″ seam allowance and press all seams in one direction (Fig. 6-3A). Set the roof aside.

3. Next, stitch four of the roof peak strips together. Press all the seams flat. Then place the roof cutting template on the strips, trace the pattern onto the fabric, and cut (Fig. 6-3A).

4. Join the roof peak to the roof section (Fig. 6-3B). Press the seams toward the roof section. Set the roof aside. Now you are ready to work on the bottom of the cottage.

5. To create the siding for either side of the door, pin together and stitch two sets of five 1½″ × 2½″ strips of Fabric 1. Press all seams in the same direction. Sew a siding section to each side of the door making sure that the seams are all pressed in the same direction. Press the door seams toward the door. Next sew a 1½″ × 6½″ strip to the end of the door and siding unit. This will become the top of the door side of the cottage (Figs. 6-3C and D). Press the seam so that it matches the other siding seams. Set aside.

Cottage Placemats and *Tea Cozy* were made from the same pattern. The irregular shape helps to add interest.

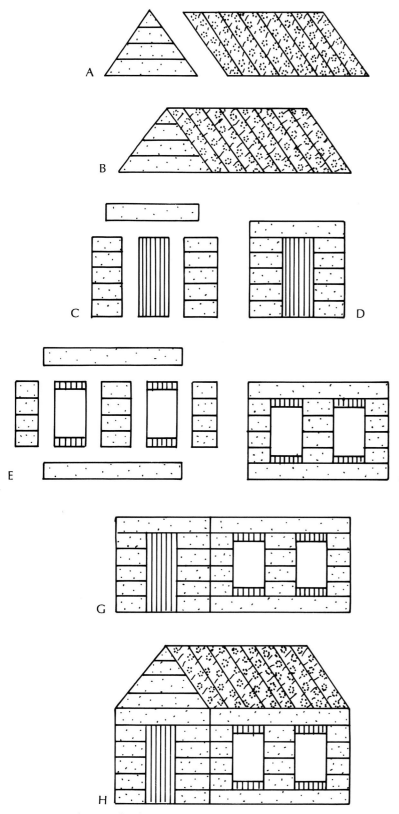

Fig. 6-3. Piecing diagram for the cottage.

6. Pin together and sew the window trim strips to the top and bottom of the two windows. Press the seams toward the trim sections. Set aside. Then take eight 1½″ × 2″ strips of Fabric 1 and sew into two sections of four. Press the seams in the same direction. Next stitch four 1½″ × 2½″ strips of Fabric 1 together to make the section between the windows (Fig. 6-3E). Press all seams in the same direction.

7. Sew the window sections to each side of the 1½″ × 2½″ section of siding. Then sew the two 1½″ × 2″ siding sections to the outside of the windows making sure that all the seams have been pressed in the same direction. Press all the vertical seams toward the windows. Now sew a 1½″ × 9½″ strip of Fabric 1 to the top and bottom of this window side section (Fig. 6-3F). Press all horizontal seams in the same direction.

8. Now you can sew the door side section to the window side section. Pin the two sections at the seam intersections so they will align. Make sure all seams are pressed in the same direction before stitching (Fig. 6-3G). Press the vertical seam flat.

9. Match the roof/peak section to the door/window section matching at the seams (Fig. 6-3H). Press the seam flat.

10. At this point you can add some embroidery stitches to represent flowering vines, or leave the cottage plain. Quilt and bind as desired. Refer to Chapter Three, Quilting Basics.

Tea Cozy

The tea cozy is constructed by making two placemats and putting a binding strip at the bottom of each one. Lay the two placemats back to back and bind the sides and tops of the cottages together. Fold the binding under at the beginning and end to give it a finished edge (Fig. 6-4).

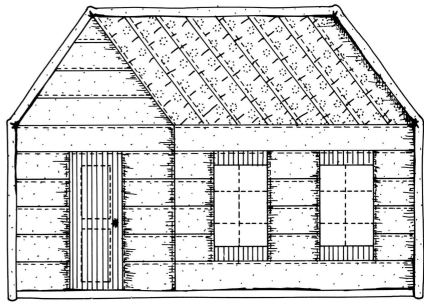

Fig. 6-4. Bind two placemats together to make the tea cozy.

Pinwheel Quilt

(Finished dimensions: 36″ × 48″.)

This quilt is a good example of how patterns can be formed by using only triangles. All you need is a template for a 3″ triangle in order to make this quilt. The design emerges in how you put the triangles together.

Fabric Requirements

Fabric 1: ½ yard of multi-colored floral print
Fabric 2: ½ yard of pale blue and white print
Fabric 3: ½ yard of blue print
Fabric 4: 1 yard of medium blue and white print
Fabric 5: 1½ yards of medium blue solid

Quantities Needed

3″ triangles: cut 48 of Fabric 1, 48 of Fabric 2, 96 of Fabric 3, 192 of Fabric 4
Backing: cut from Fabric 5
Binding: cut from Fabric 4

1. Prewash and dry the fabrics, then iron flat. Place the template on the fabrics, trace the patterns on each fabric, and cut out all the triangles.

2. Begin piecing the quilt top by joining one triangle of Fabric 4 with one triangle each of Fabrics 1, 2, and 3 along the long side of the triangle (Fig. 6-5A). Stitch, using a ¼″ seam allowance, and press all the seams to the darker side.

3. Continue by pinning two Fabric 4/Fabric 1 square combinations together (Fig. 6-5B). Stitch and press the seam allowance to one side. Repeat the process, creating five more pairs. Pin, matching all the seams.

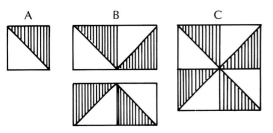

A   B   C

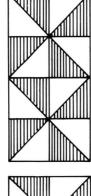

Fig. 6-5. Four pieced squares make up each pinwheel.

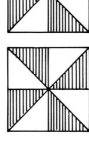

Fig. 6-6. Piece three pinwheels together to form the center section of the quilt.

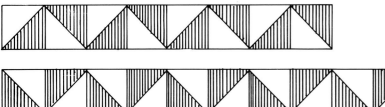

Fig. 6-7. Pieced squares sewn in a row make up one of the rounds of blocks.

Fig. 6-8. Piecing diagram for the pinwheel quilt.

Stitch together to create one pinwheel square (Fig. 6-5C). Repeat, making a total of three Fabric 4/Fabric 1 pinwheels. Sew the three pinwheels together, using a ¼″ seam allowance, matching all seams (Fig. 6-6). Press the entire center section flat.

4. Pin and then stitch together four single rows of the Fabric 4/Fabric 1 square combinations, alternating the colors (Fig. 6-7). Sew two rows of eight squares and two rows of ten squares. Press the seam allowances to one side and set these strips aside.

5. Stitch together the remaining square combinations as described above. Sew Fabric 4/Fabric 2 and Fabric 4/Fabric 3 combinations into pinwheels as shown and press each pinwheel flat.

6. Next stitch, matching and pinning at the seams, three Fabric 4/Fabric 2 pinwheels. Repeat with the remaining Fabric 4/Fabric 2 pinwheels, creating a total of four pinwheel strips. Match one of the strips to the long side of the center section and sew. Repeat with another strip on the opposite side of the center section. Pin the last two strips to the center section (Fig. 6-8), sew together, and press the new seams flat.

The pattern in this quilt was created using only triangles. It could be used as a baby quilt or a wall quilt as shown.

7. Pin, matching the seams, one of the ten-square Fabric 4/Fabric 1 strips to the long side of the center section. Sew and then press the seam allowance to one side. Repeat on the opposite side with the other ten-square strip. Stitch the two eight-square strips, matching all the seams, to the opposite ends of the center section and press the seams flat.

8. Finish piecing the quilt top by stitching together six pinwheels of Fabric 4/Fabric 3. Match the pinwheels at the seams, sew, and press

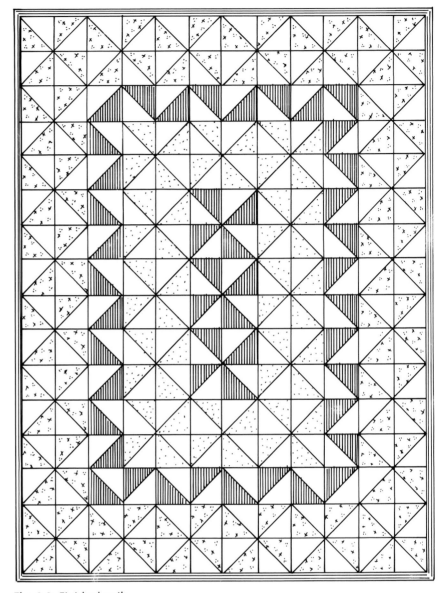

Fig. 6-9. Finished quilt.

the new seam allowances to one side. Repeat with the remaining pinwheels. Then pin one strip to the long side of the quilt top and stitch. Repeat on the opposite side of the quilt top and sew the remain-

ing two strips to the remaining edges. Stitch and press the entire quilt top flat.

9. Quilt or tie as desired and bind to finish the quilt (Fig. 6-9). Refer to Chapter Three, Quilting Basics.

Off-Center Trip Around the World Quilt

(Finished dimensions: 54" square.)

A subtle shift in a traditional quilt pattern helps to add interest. In this pattern, the shift to off-center keeps the quilt from being too static or symmetrical and makes the pattern seem more complicated than it is. This quilt is probably one of the easiest quilts to piece together, since it is made entirely of squares all the same size.

Fabric Requirements

Fabric 1: ¾ yard of white and burgundy print
Fabric 2: ¾ yard of burgundy print
Fabric 3: 2¾ yards of blue print
Fabric 4: ¾ yard of black solid

Quantities Needed

3" squares: cut 83 of Fabric 1, 81 of Fabric 2, 80 of Fabric 3, 80 of Fabric 4
Backing: cut from Fabric 3
Binding: make 6¼ yards of binding from Fabric 3

1. Prewash and dry the fabrics, then iron flat. Place the template on each color of fabric, mark patterns, and cut out the number of squares needed.

2. The easiest way to piece this quilt is to do one row at a time, piecing the squares in pairs first (Fig. 6-10). For example, the first row can be pieced in the following pairs:

(1,4) (3,2) (1,4) (3,2) (1,4) (3,2) (1,2) (3,4) (1,2)

3. Now the pairs can be pieced into groups of four:

(1,4,3,2) (1,4,3,2) (1,4,3,2) (1,2,3,4)

4. One extra pair (1,2) will be left-over, which can be attached on the end later. Sew the groups of four into groups of eight:

(1,4,3,2,1,4,3,2) (1,4,3,2,1,2,3,4)

5. Sew these two groups together and sew the extra 1,2 pair to the end of the row. Press the seams flat in the same direction. Do the same with the other rows, using the piecing diagram to show what order to piece the squares. Once all the rows have been pieced, start at the top of

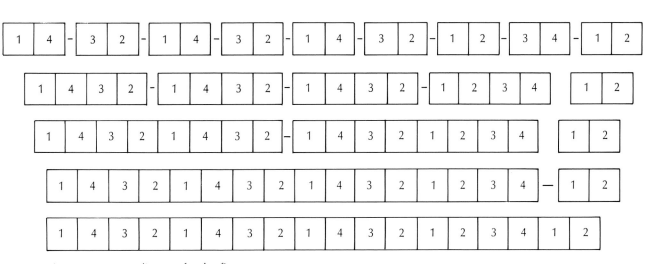

Fig. 6-10. Piecing diagram for the first row.

1	4	3	2	1	4	3	2	1	4	3	2	1	2	3	4	1	2
4	3	2	1	4	3	2	1	4	3	2	1	4	1	2	3	4	1
3	2	1	4	3	2	1	4	3	2	1	4	3	4	1	2	3	4
2	1	4	3	2	1	4	3	2	1	4	3	2	3	4	1	2	3
1	4	3	2	1	4	3	2	1	4	3	2	1	2	3	4	1	2
4	3	2	1	4	3	2	1	4	3	2	1	1	1	2	3	4	1
1	4	3	2	1	4	3	2	1	4	3	2	1	2	3	4	1	2
2	1	4	3	2	1	4	3	2	1	4	3	2	3	4	1	2	3
3	2	1	4	3	2	1	4	3	2	1	4	3	4	1	2	3	4
4	3	2	1	4	3	2	1	4	3	2	1	4	1	2	3	4	1
1	4	3	2	1	4	3	2	1	4	3	2	1	2	3	4	1	2
2	1	4	3	2	1	4	3	2	1	4	3	2	3	4	1	2	3
3	2	1	4	3	2	1	4	3	2	1	4	3	4	1	2	3	4
4	3	2	1	4	3	2	1	4	3	2	1	4	1	2	3	4	1
1	4	3	2	1	4	3	2	1	4	3	2	1	2	3	4	1	2
2	1	4	3	2	1	4	3	2	1	4	3	2	3	4	1	2	3
3	2	1	4	3	2	1	4	3	2	1	4	3	4	1	2	3	4
4	3	2	1	4	3	2	1	4	3	2	1	4	1	2	3	4	1

Fig. 6-11. Piecing diagram for the entire quilt.

the quilt and piece the rows together. Pin the rows at the seams to be sure they align when sewn. Continue this until all of the rows are pieced together (Fig. 6-11). Press the pieced quilt flat.

6. Quilt as desired and bind to complete the quilt (Fig 6-12). Refer to Chapter Three, Quilting Basics.

Quilts do not have to lay square on the table. Here the *Off-Center Trip Around the World Quilt* is canted to give a casual appearance to the table.

Fig. 6-12. Finished quilt.

Interlocking Quilt

(Finished dimensions: 46" × 58".)

This pattern gives the illusion of being more complicated than it is because of the way the colors work to form interlocking rings and because of the irregular edge. This quilt is made up of 6" blocks that, when placed correctly, together form the interlocking pattern.

Fabric Requirements

Fabric 1: 3 yards of olive green print
Fabric 2: ½ yard of rust print
Fabric 3: 4 yards of beige print
Fabric 4: ¾ yard of tan and blue print

Quantities Needed

2" triangles: cut 104 of Fabric 1, 48 of Fabric 2
2" × 4" rectangles: cut 48 of Fabric 1, 48 of Fabric 2, 14 of Fabric 4
2" × 6" rectangles: cut 32 of Fabric 1
Hexagons: cut 8 of Fabric 3, 24 of Fabric 4
2" squares: cut 7 of Fabric 3, 10 of Fabric 4
Backing: cut from Fabric 3
Binding: make 8 yards of binding from Fabric 1

1. Prewash and dry the fabrics, then iron flat. Place the templates on each color of fabric, mark patterns, and cut out. To make this quilt, first make several 6" blocks as directed below (Fig. 6-13).

2. Units A: take ten hexagons of Fabric 4 and 40 triangles of Fabric 1, and sew with right sides together, the long side of the triangles to the corners of the hexagon, using a ¼" seam allowance. The triangles' ends should extend over the hexagon approximately ¼". Press the seams toward the hexagon. Repeat this process on the other nine hexagons.

3. Unit B: Take six hexagons of Fabric 3 and 24 triangles of Fabric

2. Unit C: Take two hexagons of Fabric 3 and eight triangles of Fabric 1. Now create 6" blocks as you did in Step 2. Continue until all are finished.

4. Unit D: You will need ten hexagons of Fabric 4, 20 triangles of Fabric 1, and 20 triangles of Fabric 2. Sew the triangles to the hexagons as you did above. Repeat with the other nine hexagons.

5. Unit E: Take four hexagons of Fabric 4, 12 triangles of Fabric 1, and four triangles of Fabric 2. Sew the triangles to the hexagon as you did above. Repeat with the other three hexagons.

6. Unit F: You will need ten 2" squares of Fabric 4, twenty 2" × 4" rectangles of Fabric 1, and twenty 2" × 4" rectangles of Fabric 2. Sew a 2" square of Fabric 4 to one of the Fabric 1 rectangles, leaving ¼" unstitched on the 2" block (Fig. 6-14). Press open with the seam allowance toward the 2" block. Now sew a rectangle of Fabric 2 to this unit (Fig. 6-15A). Press open with the seam allowance toward the Fabric 2 rectangle. Next sew another Fabric 1 rectangle onto this unit (Fig. 6-

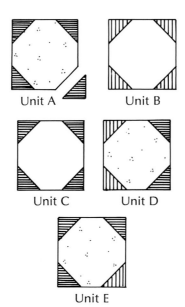

Fig. 6-13. Piecing diagram for Units A, B, C, D, and E.

Unit A   Unit B
Unit C   Unit D
Unit E

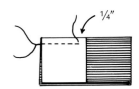

Fig. 6-14. Leave ¼" unstitched when beginning to piece Units F and G.

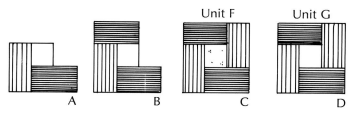

Fig. 6-15. Piecing diagram for Units F and G.

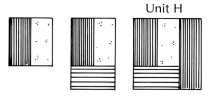

Unit H

Fig. 6-16. Piecing diagram for Unit H.

Unit I

Fig. 6-17. Piecing diagram for Unit I.

Unit I		Unit I		Unit I		Unit I
Unit E	Unit H	Unit D	Unit H	Unit D	Unit H	Unit E
Unit H	Unit A	Unit F	Unit A	Unit F	Unit A	Unit H
Unit D	Unit F	Unit B	Unit G	Unit B	Unit F	Unit D
Unit H	Unit A	Unit G	Unit C	Unit G	Unit A	Unit H
Unit D	Unit F	Unit B	Unit G	Unit B	Unit F	Unit D
Unit H	Unit A	Unit G	Unit C	Unit G	Unit A	Unit H
Unit D	Unit F	Unit B	Unit G	Unit B	Unit F	Unit D
Unit H	Unit A	Unit F	Unit A	Unit F	Unit A	Unit H
Unit E	Unit H	Unit D	Unit H	Unit D	Unit H	Unit E
Unit I		Unit I		Unit I		Unit I

Fig. 6-18. Piecing diagram for the entire quilt.

15B). Press open with seam allowance toward the Fabric 1 rectangle. Sew the second Fabric 2 rectangle to this unit to finish the block. First sew the long side of the rectangle to the rest of the block. The ¼" you left unstitched earlier will make it possible for doing this. At the corner turn the block in your sewing machine and stitch the short side (Fig 6-15C). Press the block flat. Do the same with the other nine blocks.

7. Unit G: You will need seven 2" squares of Fabric 3, fourteen 2" × 4" rectangles of Fabric 1, and fourteen 2" × 4" rectangles of Fabric 2. Follow the instructions for making Unit F replacing the Fabric 4 squares with Fabric 3 squares (Fig. 6-15D). Repeat with the other six blocks.

8. Unit H: You will need fourteen 2" × 4" rectangles of Fabric 4, fourteen 2" × 4" rectangles of Fabric 1, fourteen 2" × 4" rectangles of Fabric 2, and fourteen 2" × 6" rectangles of Fabric 1. Sew a 2" × 4" rectangle of Fabric 1 to a 2" × 4" rectangle of Fabric 4. Press flat with the seam allowance toward Fabric 1. Sew a 2" × 4" rectangle of Fabric 2 to the end of the Fabric 1/Fabric 4 rectangle. Press flat with the seam allowance toward Fabric 2. Attach the 2" × 6" rectangle of Fabric 1 to the long side of this unit. Press flat with the seam allowance toward Fabric 1 (Fig. 6-16). Continue until all 14 blocks are finished.

9. Unit I: You will need eight 2" × 6" rectangles of Fabric 1 and 16 triangles of Fabric 1. Sew a triangle to each end of the rectangle (Fig. 6-17). Press flat with the seam allowance toward the rectangle.

10. Now piece together the rows, following the piecing diagram, to assemble the units (Fig. 6-18). Add

This *Interlocking Quilt* works as a throw for keeping you warm on cold days. The irregular edge adds interest to the quilt, but this pattern can be finished off square if preferred.

Fig. 6-19. Finished quilt.

either a 2″ × 6″ rectangle of Fabric 1 or triangles of Fabric 1 to the ends of the row as shown. On the top and bottom of the quilt attach the eight I Units in place. When piecing the rows together, pin to match each seam from row to row so that the block will align properly.

11. When you have finished piecing, either quilt or tie the quilt as desired (Fig. 6-19). Refer to Chapter Three, Quilting Basics.

Shower Curtain

(Finished dimensions: 72″ square, not including the strip used for hanging.)

A quilted shower curtain? Such a quilt gives your bathroom personality, and you can control the colors you wish to use instead of having to settle for the shower curtains available at your local department store.

There are two things to remember when doing this project: Use flannel in place of batting to keep down the thickness and put a plastic liner between the quilt and the shower. As an extra precaution, you can also back the shower curtain in waterproof nylon.

Fabric Requirements

Fabric 1: 1 yard of maize and pale blue print
Fabric 2: 1 yard of maize and pale blue print
Fabric 3: 1 yard of medium green print
Fabric 4: 1 yard of dark green print
Fabric 5: 3½ yards of medium blue print
Fabric 6: 1 yard of dark blue print
Fabric 7: 5 yards, minimum 44″-wide fabric of green print
Batting: 5 yards, lightweight flannel, minimum 44″-wide fabric

Quantities Needed

4″ triangles: cut 56 of Fabric 1, 56 of Fabric 2, 36 of Fabric 3, 36 of Fabric 4, 88 of Fabric 5, 88 of Fabric 6
4″ squares: cut 14 of Fabric 1, 14 of Fabric 2, 36 of Fabric 3, 36 of Fabric 4, 31 of Fabric 5, 31 of Fabric 6
Backing: cut from Fabric 7
Binding: make 6½ yards of binding from Fabric 5

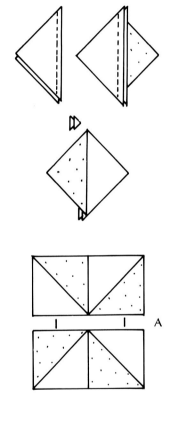

1. Prewash and dry the fabrics, then iron flat. Place the templates on each color of fabric, mark patterns, and cut out all of the squares and triangles.

2. Join one triangle each of Fabrics 1 and 2 along the long edge, with right sides together. Stitch, using a ¼″ seam allowance, and press the seam to one side. Repeat, creating three more of the pieced squares. Pin together two of the pieced squares, with right sides together, matching Fabric 1 to Fabric 2, and sew. Do the same with the other pieced squares. Press all seam al-

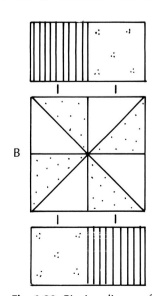

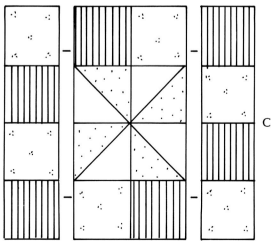

Fig. 6-20. Piecing diagram for the center of the quilt.

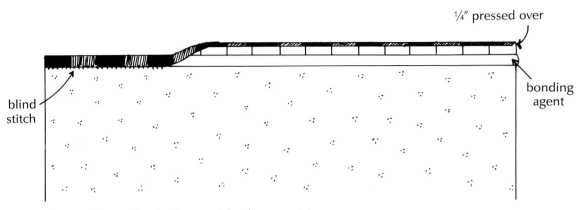

Fig. 6-21. Preparation for the top of the shower curtain.

Fig. 6-22. Finished shower curtain.

lowances to one side. Next pin the pieces, matching the seams, and sew, using a ¼″ seam allowance (Fig. 6-20A). Press the center square flat and set aside.

3. Join together all of the remaining triangle pieces, sewing on the long edge of each pair to create the re-

maining pieced squares. Match the Fabric 1 and 2 triangles, the Fabric 3 and 4 triangles, and the Fabric 5

Not only does a quilted shower curtain provide a focal point to your bathroom but it acts as a conversation piece as well.

and 6 triangles. Sew each together, press the seam allowances to one side, and set aside.

4. Sew two alternating pieces of Fabrics 3 and 4 together to create a pair. Repeat to create a total of six pairs. Pin one pair to one side of the center square, with right sides together and matching seams, and a second to the opposite side of the center square (Fig. 6-20B). Press all the seams toward the darker fabric. Next sew two of the remaining pairs of alternating fabrics together and press seams flat. Repeat with the last two pairs. Pin the two strips to opposite sides of the center square, matching all the seams, and alternating the fabrics around the entire center square (Fig. 6-20C). Stitch and press the block flat.

5. Repeat this process with each succeeding round in the following order: Fabrics 3 and 4 pieced squares, Fabrics 1 and 2 squares, Fabrics 5 and 6 pieced squares, Fabrics 3 and 4 squares, Fabrics 1 and 2 pieced squares, Fabrics 3 and 4 squares. End with Fabrics 5 and 6 pieced squares as the last row around the edge. Press the entire quilt top flat and set aside.

6. To create the backing fabric, sew two equal-size pieces of Fabric 7 with right sides together (approximately 2½ yards for each piece). Press the seam open and press the entire backing piece flat. Place backing fabric on the floor or a large table, wrong side up, and center a piece of flannel batting fabric, of approximately the same size, onto the backing fabric. Center the shower curtain top over both the backing and batting pieces and baste the layers together. Quilt or tie as desired.

7. Next, stitch together nine squares each of both Fabrics 5 and 6 into a single strip of alternating blocks. Press all seam allowances in one direction. Press one side of strip over ¼", with wrong sides together. Pin the strip onto one side of the curtain top, matching the seams and pinning through all layers. Stitch together using a ¼" seam and press the seam toward the top strip. Cut a length of a fabric stabilizer or bonding agent 1½" × 72" long and place on the wrong side of the attached strip, on the side nearest the quilted curtain (Fig. 6-21). Fold the other side of the strip over, matching the ironed edge

with the line of stitching. Press, bonding the strip together as suggested by the product manufacturer, and then blind stitch the strip to the backing.

8. To finish, cut off excess backing and batting fabrics, trimming both even with edges of the curtain top. Set this aside and sew binding strips together to create a total of 6½ yards of binding. Fold over one edge of the binding ¼", with wrong sides together, and press.

9. Pin, with right sides together, the unpressed edge of the binding strip to three sides of the curtain top. Stitch the binding to the top, leaving ¼" extra on each unfinished end. Fold over and press under the extra ¼". Fold the binding to the back and hand sew, using a blind stitch, to finish the binding.

10. Lay the entire curtain flat and mark 12 buttonholes on the top strip, beginning 1" from each edge. Space the remaining holes equally along the length of the top strip. Machine sew the buttonholes, beginning ½" from the top edge and clip each to open. Hang on a shower rod with purchased shower-curtain rings (Fig. 6-22).

CHAPTER SEVEN

Decorative Quilts

Wild Blue Rose Quilt

(Finished Dimensions: 34" square.)

This quilt is a good project for beginners. It is made from a combination of squares and triangles, which are the basis for many traditional patterns. The quilt shown uses moire taffeta for the pink areas, but the first-time quilter should work with a stable fabric such as cotton before branching out into taffeta or satin, which are slippery and tend to ravel.

Here the *Wild Blue Rose Quilt* hangs in a living room. Even though this is a tied quilt, the fabrics used, including a moire taffeta, make it appropriate for a formal setting.

Fabric Requirements

Fabric 1: ¼ yard of white
Fabric 2: ½ yard of pink moire taffeta
Fabric 3: 1¾ yards of navy blue solid
Fabric 4: ½ yard of navy blue and pink rose floral

Quantities Needed

Center section
3″ squares: cut 8 of Fabric 3, 8 of Fabric 4, 16 of Fabric 1
3″ triangles: cut 32 of Fabric 1, 32 of Fabric 2

Pieced border
2″ squares: cut 60 of Fabric 3, 60 of Fabric 4

Inside border
Fabric 2: cut 2 strips 1½″ × 24½″ and 2 strips 1½″ × 26½″

Note: The inside border strips do not need a template, and the dimensions given include ¼″ seam allowance on all sides.

Backing: cut from Fabric 3
Binding: make 4 yards of binding from Fabric 2

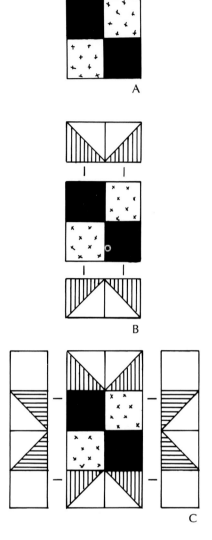

1. Prewash and dry fabrics, then iron flat. If you are using any special fabrics or "glamour" fabrics such as taffeta or satin, prepare these fabrics as suggested by the manufacturer or as noted on the fabric bolt. Place templates on the fabrics and trace the patterns onto each fabric. Then cut out all the squares and triangles required.

2. The center section of this quilt has four pieced blocks. Begin creating one block by joining, with right sides together, one 3″ square of Fabric 3 and one 3″ square of Fabric 4. Repeat with a second set of squares in Fabrics 3 and 4. Pin together at the seams, matching one square of Fabric 3 with one square of Fabric 4. This will make a 6″

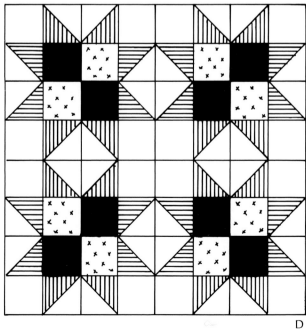

Fig. 7-1. Piecing diagram for the center block.

pieced square. Stitch, using a ¼″ seam allowance, and press the squares flat (Fig. 7-1A). Next, matching long sides of the 3″ triangles, stitch one triangle of Fabric 1 and one triangle of Fabric 2, with right sides together, and press the seam allowances toward the darker fabric. Repeat until eight 3″ pieced squares are created.

3. Join two 3″ pieced squares together, matching the short sides of Fabric 1, to form a rectangle. Press the seam allowances to one side. Repeat to make a total of four rectangles. Pin one rectangle to a side of the 6″ pieced squares, orienting it so that the triangle points are pointing away from the center square, matching seams (Fig. 7-1B). Sew, using a ¼″ seam allowance. Repeat on the opposite side of the 6″ pieced square. Press all the seam allowances toward the rectangles. Attach one 3″ square of Fabric 1 to the short side of one of the Fabric 1/ Fabric 2 rectangles. Repeat process on the opposite side of the rectangle to create a strip. Repeat with the last rectangle and the two 3″ Fabric 1 squares. Stitch together with a ¼″ seam allowance and press the seams toward the outside (Fig. 7-1C). Set aside completed block and repeat entire process to make at total of four blocks.

4. To complete the center section, pin together two center blocks, matching the seams, and stitch, using a ¼″ seam allowance. Press the seam flat. Repeat with the other two center blocks. Finally, pin together the last two pieces, matching all seams. Stitch, using a ¼″ seam, and press the entire center section flat (Fig. 7-1D).

5. Pin the long edge of one 1½″ × 24½″ inside border strip to one side of the center section, with right sides together. Stitch, and press the

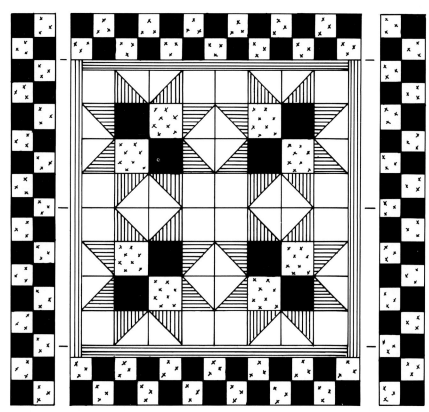

Fig. 7-2. Piecing diagram for *Wild Blue Rose Quilt.*

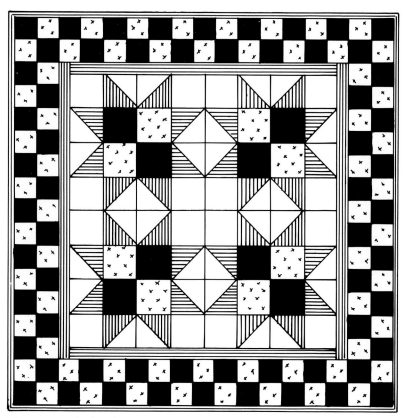

Fig. 7-3. Finished quilt.

seam allowance toward the inside border strip. Repeat with the other 1½″ × 24½″ border strip, attaching the piece opposite the first strip, and press the seam allowance toward the inside border strip. Pin the last two inside border strips (1½″ × 26½″) to the remaining sides of the center section, with right sides together. Stitch together and press seams toward the border strips. Set aside the center section.

6. To create the pieced border, stitch together the 2″ squares, beginning and ending with Fabric 3, and alternating Fabric 3 and Fabric 4 to make a strip of 17 squares. Sew a second strip of 17 squares, beginning and ending with a 2″ square of Fabric 4. Press the seam allowances toward the dark fabric. Match the

two strips at all seams and pin. Sew the strips together and press the seam allowance to one side. Repeat this process with a second set of squares. Set aside the two sections of pieced border.

7. Sew the remaining pieced border by stitching thirteen 2″ squares, alternating the colors and beginning and ending with a square of Fabric 3 into one strip. Make a second strip of 13 squares beginning and ending with Fabric 4. Press the seam allowances toward the darker fabric. Join the two strips together, matching and pinning at all seams, and stitch, using a ¼″ seam allowance. Press the seam to one side. Repeat with the remaining 2″ squares.

8. Attach one section of the pieced border (13 squares) to the center section, as shown in the piecing diagram (Fig. 7-2). Stitch, using a ¼″ seam allowance, and press the seam toward border piece. Repeat with the second 13-square border piece, again stitching ¼″ seam and pressing seam allowance flat toward the border. Attach the two remaining border pieces to the opposite sides of the center section, matching at the seams. Pin and stitch, using a ¼″ seam allowance, being certain the colors alternate around all sides of the quilt top, as shown in the example. Press the seam allowances flat toward pieced border.

9. Quilt as desired (Fig. 7-3). Refer to Chapter Three, Quilting Basics.

Spectrum Rail Fence Quilt

(Finished dimensions: 42″ square.)

This quilt is a traditional pattern with a new twist: A combination of large and small blocks sets this quilt apart from its traditional counterparts. The use of bright colors, seen in the photograph, makes a very strong statement; however, you can tone the quilt down by using colors that are more muted and closer in value.

Fabric Requirements

Fabric 1: ½ yard of yellow solid
Fabric 2: ½ yard of orange solid
Fabric 3: ½ yard of red solid
Fabric 4: ½ yard of purple solid
Fabric 5: ½ yard of blue solid
Fabric 6: ½ yard of green solid
Fabric 7: 2 yards of black solid
Fabric 8: ½ yard of white solid

Quantities Needed

1″ × 3″ rectangle: cut 32 from Fabric 1, 32 from Fabric 2, 32 from Fabric 3, 32 from Fabric 4, 32 from Fabric 5, 32 from Fabric 6

2″ × 6″ rectangle: cut 10 from Fabric 1, 10 from Fabric 2, 10 from Fabric 3, 10 from Fabric 4, 10 from Fabric 5, 10 from Fabric 6

Inside border: cut from Fabric 8, 2 pieces 1½″ × 38½″, and 2 pieces 1½″ × 36½″

Outside border: cut from Fabric 7, 2 pieces 2½″ × 42½″, and 2 pieces 2½″ × 38½″

Backing: cut from Fabric 7

Binding: cut from Fabric 7

Note: In sewing together the 3″ and 6″ pieced squares that make up the blocks in this project, piece together each square from dark to medium to light. Fabrics 1, 2, and 3 make up one block and Fabrics 4, 5, and 6 make up another block. Also, in piecing together each of the nine blocks in this design, orient the squares sewn from Fabrics 1, 2, and 3 vertically and those from Fabrics 4, 5, and 6 horizontally.

1. Prewash and dry the fabrics, then iron flat. Place the templates on each color of fabric, mark the patterns, and cut out the required number of rectangles.

2. Begin sewing the quilt top by stitching together all 1″ × 3″ rectangles as described above, to create 64 pieced squares. Press each of the seams toward the darker fabric and set aside the 3″ pieced squares. Next do the same with the 2″ × 6″ rectangles, to make 20 pieced squares, 6″ × 6″ square (Fig. 7-4A).

3. Join together, in rows of four, the 3″ pieced squares (Fig. 7-4B). Then pin, matching seams, four of the rows, alternating colors to make one block. Press all seam allowances in one direction. Repeat with the remaining rows of four, to create a total of four blocks. Set aside blocks.

4. Pin together the 6″ pieced squares (Fig. 7-4C). Stitch into two square rows, and then sew together, matching seams, two rows to create a block. Press the seams in one direction and repeat the process to make a total of five blocks.

5. Sew three blocks together to form the top row, matching seams (Fig. 7-4D). Stitch, using a ¼″ seam allowance, and press seams to one side. Repeat to create the remaining two rows. Join rows together, matching the seams. Stitch and press quilt top flat.

6. Pin 1½″ × 36½″ inside border strips, with right sides together, to the opposite sides of the quilt top. Stitch and press the seams toward the quilt top. Next sew 1½″ × 38½″ strips to the remaining two sides of quilt top, pressing the seam allowance toward the quilt top. Repeat with the outside border strips, and press the quilt top flat.

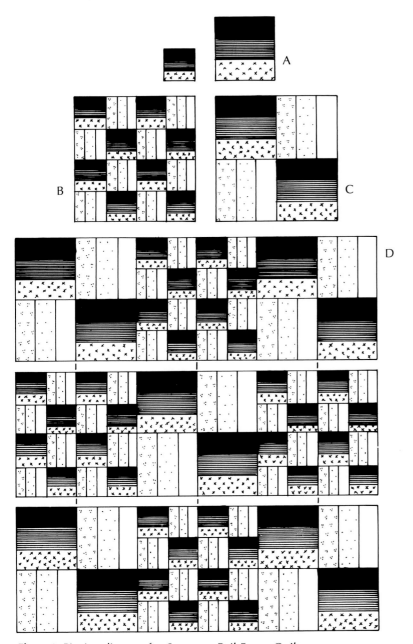

Fig. 7-4. Piecing diagram for *Spectrum Rail Fence Quilt.*

7. Assemble the backing fabric, batting, and quilt top, and baste through all layers. Quilt or tie as desired and bind the edges to complete the quilt (Fig. 7-5).

The *Spectrum Rail Fence Quilt* adds a colorful touch to an artist's work area.

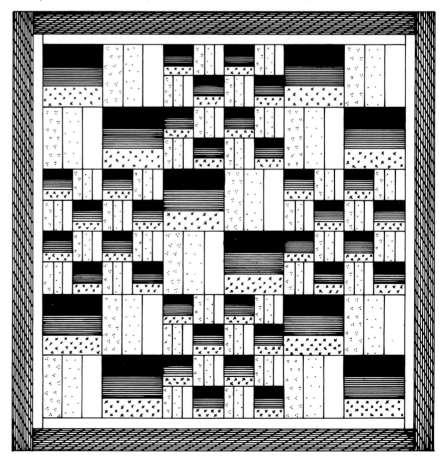

Fig. 7-5. Finished quilt.

Lone Star Quilt

(Finished dimensions: 47" square.)

The Lone Star pattern is very colorful and full of motion. Even though the pattern is a star it has a circular feel to it, and you can play off this by using it as a table cover on a round table. This version of the Lone Star has squares inserted between the points to give it its own personality and flare.

Fabric Requirements

Fabric 1: ½ yard of dark blue print
Fabric 2: ½ yard of dark green print
Fabric 3: ½ yard of maize and blue small print
Fabric 4: 3 yards of medium blue print
Fabric 5: ¼ yard of medium green print
Fabric 6: ¾ yard of maize and blue tiny print

Quantities Needed

Diamonds: cut 48 from Fabric 3, 64 from Fabric 4, 16 from Fabric 1, 40 from Fabric 5, 32 from Fabric 2
5" squares: cut 8 from Fabric 1
Background: for the corner sections, cut 8 from Fabric 6; for the triangular sections, cut 8 from Fabric 6
Outside border: cut 2 pieces from Fabric 2, 2½" × 43", and 2 pieces from Fabric 2, 2½" × 47"
Backing: cut from Fabric 4
Binding: cut from Fabric 4

Note: Instead of purchasing extra yardage of Fabric 2 for cutting the outside border pieces, cut 12 strips 2½" × 18" from the ½ yard piece and stitch together using a ¼" seam into four strips, which will measure 2½" × 53½" (Fig. 7-6). Cut the strips to the required sizes and press flat.

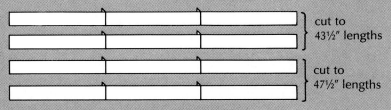

cut to 43½" lengths

cut to 47½" lengths

Fig. 7-6. Piece the border section to save fabric.

1. Prewash and dry the fabrics, then iron flat. Place the templates on each color of fabric, mark the patterns, and cut out. Also cut out all the strips required for this project.

2. To piece the quilt top, begin by piecing the points of the star. Each point consists of five rows pieced from five diamonds. Start with one diamond of Fabric 1 and join to diamond of Fabric 2 (Fig. 7-7A). Continue adding diamonds to complete the row (Fig. 7-7B). Stitch together the other four rows as shown (Fig. 7-7C). Press all seam allowances in the same direction. Pin together the rows, matching at the seams, and stitch. Press seam allowances flat. Repeat the process with the remaining diamonds, to complete eight points.

3. With right sides together, matching all the seams, join two points to make one-fourth of the center star. Stitch, leaving ¼" unsewn so that you can insert the triangular sections later. Press the seam flat. Repeat with the other star point sections for a total of four quarter sections. Next join two quarter sections to make half of the center star. Repeat with the other two quarter sections. Press both seams flat. To complete the center star, match seams of both half-star sections, and pin and stitch together. Press the seam flat and lay the center star section aside.

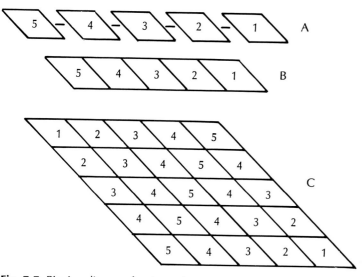

Fig. 7-7. Piecing diagram for star points.

Fig. 7-8. Finished center star.

This variation on the Lone Star pattern gives the impression of one large flower.

4. Next pin one 5″ square, with right sides together, to the short edge of one background corner piece. Stitch, stopping ¼″ from the edge on one side. Pin another background corner piece onto the other edge of the 5″ square. Stitch and press the seam allowances toward the square. With the right sides of the diagonal edges of the background corner together, stitch, stopping where the 5″ square joins the background corner. Press the seams flat. Repeat this process with the remaining three corners (Fig 7-9A).

5. Pin the background corner piece between two points of the center star, with right sides together (Fig. 7-9B). Stitch the seam, ending ¼″ from the inside corner. Press the seam toward the center star, then pin the background corner section to the other center star point. Stitch, easing the corner to fit. Press and repeat with the three other background corner sections.

6. Sew the background triangular sections next. Pin one 5″ square, with right sides together, to a background triangular section. Stitch, stopping ¼″ from the edge, as was done with the background corner sections. Pin and stitch another background triangular section to the 5″ square. To complete the triangular piece, stitch the middle seam (Fig. 7-10A). Press the seams flat. Repeat this process with the other 5″ squares and triangular background sections for a total of four triangular pieces..

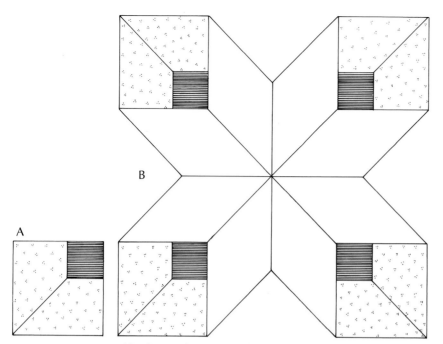

Fig. 7-9. Placement of background corner sections.

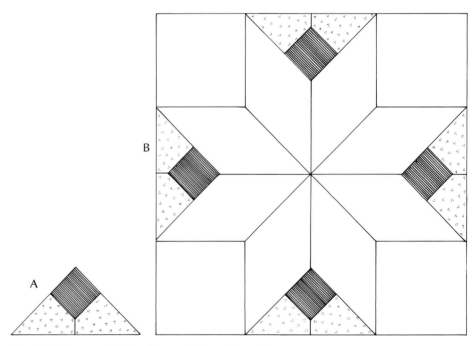

Fig. 7-10. Placement of background triangular sections.

Fig. 7-11. Finished quilt.

7. Pin one triangular background piece between two points of the center star, with right sides together. The 5″ square piece should be placed as shown in Fig. 7-10B. Stitch the seam, ending ¼″ from the inside corner. Press seam toward the center star, then pin the triangular background piece to the other center star point. Stitch, easing the corner to fit. Press and repeat with the other three triangular background pieces. Press the entire piece flat.

8. To add the border, pin, with right sides together, the shorter length of border to the quilt center. Stitch and press seams toward the border section. Repeat on the opposite side of the quilt top. Complete the quilt top by sewing on the two remaining border strips. Press the seams toward the border strips.

9. Quilt as desired and bind edges to finish the quilt (Fig. 7-11). Refer to Chapter Three, Quilting Basics.

Throw Pillow Slipcase

(Finished dimensions: to fit a 14″ square pillow.)

This project helps to spruce up older, worn throw pillows or to update a color scheme. Simply make the slipcase to fit your existing pillow.

Fabric Requirements

Fabric 1: ½ yard of mauve, green, and ivory print
Fabric 2: ½ yard of gray and mauve print
Fabric 3: ½ yard of burgundy print

Quantities Needed

Inside piece: cut 1, 16½″ square, of Fabric 2
Outside piece: cut 1 of Fabric 1
Backing: cut from Fabric 3
Binding: 3 yards of 1″ ribbon
Ties: cut 2 pieces, 18″ long, of 1″ mauve ribbon

Note: 1″ ribbon was used to bind the project shown, but it could also be done using standard bias binding of matching or contrasting fabric.

1. Prewash and dry the fabrics, then iron flat. Create a template using Fig. 7-12 as a guide and cut the outside piece.

2. To create the inside piece, cut a piece of Fabric 2, 16½″ square. Press over ¼″ on two of the opposite sides and stitch. Set aside.

3. Lay on a flat surface a piece of backing fabric, wrong side up, and place batting fabric on top. Center the outside piece over the batting and backing fabric and baste through all the layers. Quilt as desired.

4. To finish, trim even with the outside piece any excess backing fabric. Next, lay flat the quilted outside piece, with backing side up. Center the inside piece, right side up, on the outside piece, matching the raw edges. Baste the inside and outside pieces together along raw edge (Fig. 7-13). Bind edges to complete.

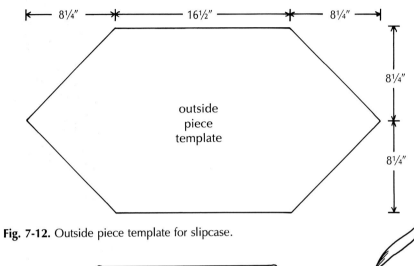

Fig. 7-12. Outside piece template for slipcase.

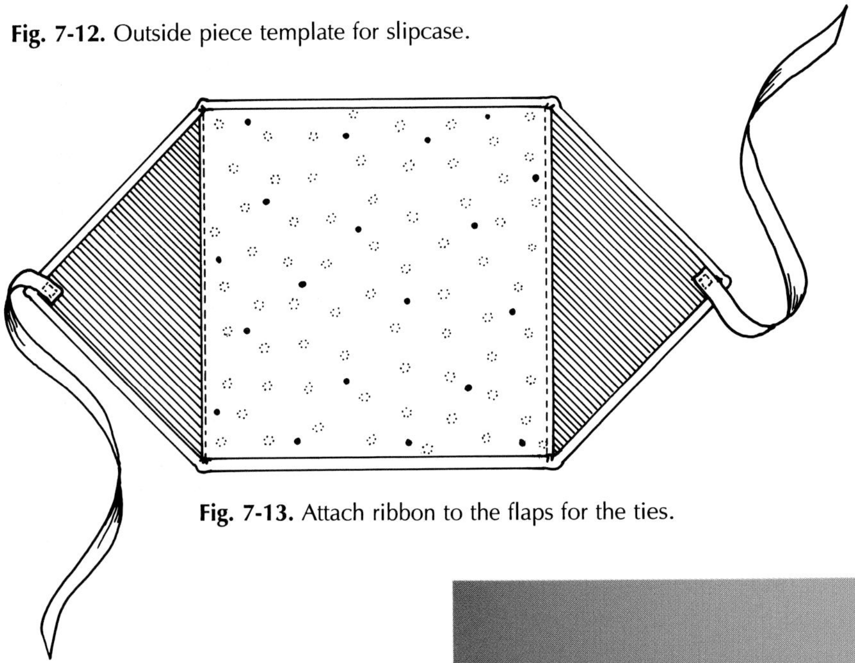

Fig. 7-13. Attach ribbon to the flaps for the ties.

This pillow slipcase can be an elegant accent in your living room or bedroom. Because of the bow, it is more for show than for everyday use.

5. Attach one length of 18″-long ribbon to the wrong side of one outside flap, hand stitching in place. Repeat with the second length of ribbon on the other outside flap.

Slip the pillow form in behind the inside piece and fold over the two outside flaps. Tie ribbon in a bow (Fig. 7-14).

Fig. 7-14. Finished pillow.

Shelf Liner

(Finished dimensions: 35½″ wide, as shown, with 6″ drop, 12″ drop at the center point.)

A shelf liner can be either decorative or useful. This pattern was designed to help hide a VCR and tape rewinder, which sit on a shelf in an armoire. Shelf liners can also be used for strictly decorative purposes. Measure the space where you want your shelf liner and adapt this pattern to the shelf size.

Note: For this project, only the front drop portion is quilted or tied, making this a quick and easy project, and perfect for the beginning quilter.

Fabric Requirements

Fabric 1: ¼ yard of olive green print
Fabric 2: ¼ yard of rust print
Fabric 3: 2½ yards of beige print

Quantities Needed

6″ triangles: cut 8 of Fabric 1, 8 of Fabric 2
Side panels: cut 2 of Fabric 3
Backing: cut from Fabric 3
Binding: cut from Fabric 3
Shelf flap: cut from Fabric 3

1. Prewash and dry all the fabrics, then iron flat. Place the templates on each color of fabric, mark patterns, and cut out the required number of pieces.

2. Piece together the center point section by pinning, with right sides together, one of the 6″ triangles of Fabric 1 and one of Fabric 2, along the short edge, to create a larger pieced triangle (Fig. 7-15A). Stitch, using a ¼″ seam allowance, and press the seams toward the darker fabric. Repeat with the remaining 6″ triangle pieces. Next join together two of the

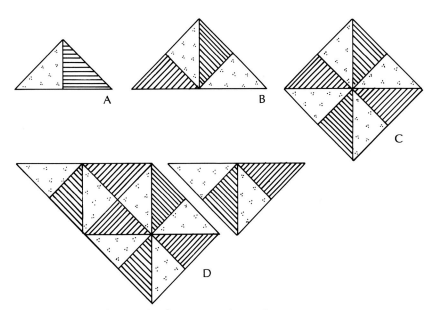

Fig. 7-15. Piecing diagram for the center point section.

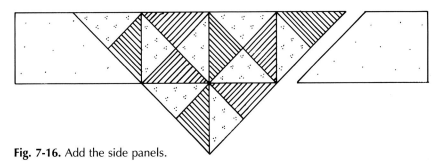

Fig. 7-16. Add the side panels.

pieced triangles, alternating the colors, and stitch (Fig. 7-15B). Press the seams to one side and repeat with the remaining two-piece triangles. Pin together two of the larger triangles to make the center pinwheel, matching center seams and alternating the colors, and stitch (Fig. 7-15C). Press the seam allowance to one side. To finish piecing the center point section, pin to the center pinwheel each of the remaining four-piece triangles, matching at the seams (Fig. 7-15D). Stitch, then press the center point section flat.

3. Next pin the two side panel sections to each side of the center point section and sew, using a ¼″ seam (Fig. 7-16). Press all seam allowances toward side panel sections.

4. To quilt, lay a piece of backing fabric flat, with wrong side up, allowing for several inches of extra fabric on all sides of the pieced shelf liner section. Center a piece of batting over the backing fabric and then, right side up, center the pieced shelf liner section. Baste all the layers together, and quilt or tie as desired.

5. After quilting or tying, lay the liner flat and trim away the excess batting and backing fabric, even with the edge of the pieced shelf liner section. Attach the binding to the edges, leaving the top edge unbound. Fold over the binding and hand stitch to the quilt back, using a blind stitch.

A shelf liner can be decorative as well as useful. Here the liner hides the VCR and tape rewinder on the shelf behind it.

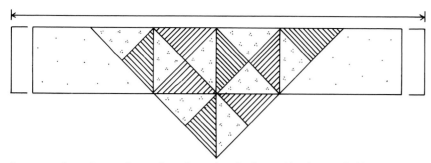

Fig. 7-17. The side panels can be adjusted to fit the width of your shelf.

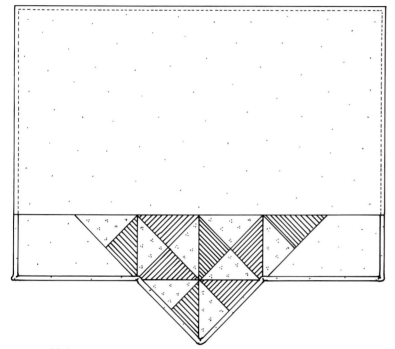

Fig. 7-18. Add the shelf flap to the drop section.

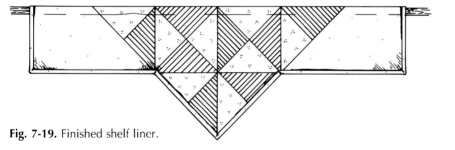

Fig. 7-19. Finished shelf liner.

6. Measure the finished top edge dimension and determine the depth required to cover the shelf surface. Add 1″ to the overall width and ¾″ to the overall depth to allow for seam allowance and edge finishing. Cut the shelf flap from Fabric 3 in the dimensions determined above.

7. Press under ¼″, wrong sides together, on the two side edges of the shelf flap and press. Fold over ¼″ again, and press and stitch close to the edge (Fig. 7-18). Repeat this process with one of the back sections to finish shelf flat edges on three sides.

8. To complete the shelf liner, pin, matching the right sides of the quilted shelf liner and shelf flap. Stitch, using a ¼″ seam (Fig. 7-19).

Christmas Tree Skirt

(Finished dimensions: 48″ diameter.)

Christmas provides a wonderful opportunity for decorating, and here is a project to help you decorate with quilts. The Christmas Tree Skirt can be easily adapted, using different colors and fabrics, to any style of decorating.

Satin, lamé, and taffeta were used in the photograph, but cotton prints can give an older or country feel to your tree skirt. You can also stencil patterns on the pieces to give it a different look. Or the 12 sections around the tree skirt can correspond to the Twelve Days of Christmas.

Fabric Requirements

Fabric 1: ½ yard of green iridescent taffeta
Fabric 2: ½ yard of red moire taffeta
Fabric 3: ½ yard of ivory satin
Fabric 4: ½ yard of ivory brocade
Fabric 5: 1 yard of gold lamé
Fabric 6: 3½ yards of red solid cotton

Quantities Needed

Inside ring: cut 6 of Fabric 1, 6 of Fabric 2
Center ring: cut 6 of Fabric 3, 6 of Fabric 4
Outside ring: cut 6 of Fabric 1, 6 of Fabric 2
Welting: cut from Fabric 5
Backing: cut from Fabric 6
Satin ruffle: 6 yards of ivory required

Note: The yardage required for this project will provide ample scraps that can be used in making the Christmas Ornaments shown on page 103, as well as the Christmas Stocking shown on page 105.

1. Prepare all fabrics according to the manufacturer's directions. If using "glamour" fabrics such as taffeta, satin, or lamé, prewashing is not necessary. If the tree skirt becomes soiled with use, dry-cleaning the finished piece is preferred over machine washing. If using calicoes or other typical quilting fabrics, prewashing is recommended. Press all the fabrics flat, and place templates on each fabric to be used. Trace patterns on all fabrics, and cut all the required pieces. Set scraps aside for later use.

2. Begin sewing the tree skirt top by pinning along the lower curved edge of one of the inside ring pieces and the upper curved edge of one of the center ring pieces. Match all Fabric 2 inside ring pieces with all Fabric 3 center ring pieces, and all Fabric 1 pieces to all Fabric 4 pieces. Stitch, using a ¼″ seam allowance, clip curves, and press the seams toward the darker fabric (Fig. 7-20). Next pin together the long straight edges of the inner ring/center ring pieces, alternating the colors, and stitch, using a ¼″ seam allowance. Leave the last edge and the first edge unsewn, to create an opening (Fig. 7-21). Set aside the inside/center section.

3. Sew together the welting as described in Chapter Three, Quilting Basics. Set aside welting. Next, with right sides together along the

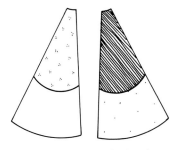

Fig. 7-20. Pieced panels for the inside center ring.

The *Christmas Tree Skirt* helps to carry the quilt theme throughout your holiday decorating. This skirt was made from satin, lamé, and taffeta fabrics.

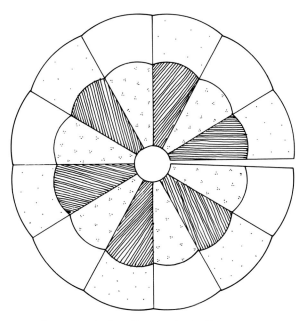

Fig. 7-21. Piecing diagram for inside center ring.

straight edge, pin together one piece of the outside ring in Fabric 1 and one of Fabric 2, and sew. Repeat, alternating the colors, and leaving an opening after the last piece (Fig. 7-22). Press all seam allowances in one direction. Set aside the outside ring.

4. Pin the welting to the right side of inside/center ring along the lower curved edge. Baste, and then pin, with right side down, the top curved edge of the outside ring to the inside/center ring. Stitch through all layers, using a zipper foot, as close as possible to the cord of the welting. Clip curves and press the seam allowances toward the darker fabric.

5. To finish, lay the backing fabric, right side down, on a flat surface. Over the backing, center the quilt top, right side up, and baste all layers together. Quilt or tie as desired. Trim away excess fabric. Sew ruffle around the edge of the tree skirt and press seam allowance toward the skirt. Bind remaining edges to complete the tree skirt (Fig. 7-23).

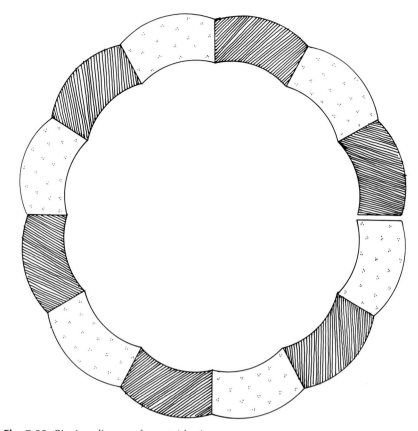

Fig. 7-22. Piecing diagram for outside ring.

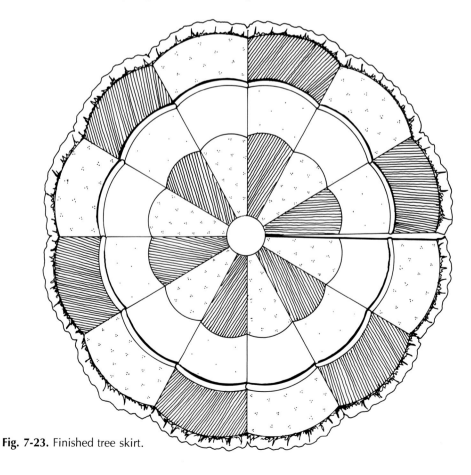

Fig. 7-23. Finished tree skirt.

Christmas Ornaments

Even your Christmas tree can be decked out in quilted splendor. Here are instructions for making three different quilted ornaments. Two of the ornaments can be as a holding device for items such as flowers, cinnamon sticks, and candy canes. The other ornament is for a tufted star, which sparkles when made out of lamé.

Fabric Requirements

You can use scraps of fabric from the other Christmas projects in this book depending on how many ornaments you need. Or buy ¼ yard each of a few fabrics and make as many ornaments as you can.

Cornucopia and Sling Ornaments

1. Prewash and dry the fabrics, then iron flat. You will need two 4″ squares for each ornament you wish to make (see template). It is recommended that you use two different fabrics for a more festive look.

2. Place two 4″ squares of fabric, with right sides together, on your work surface. Put a 4″ square of batting on top of this and stitch around the edge of the square leaving a 1½″ opening. Turn the square inside out and press flat. Blind stitch the opening closed (Fig. 7-24).

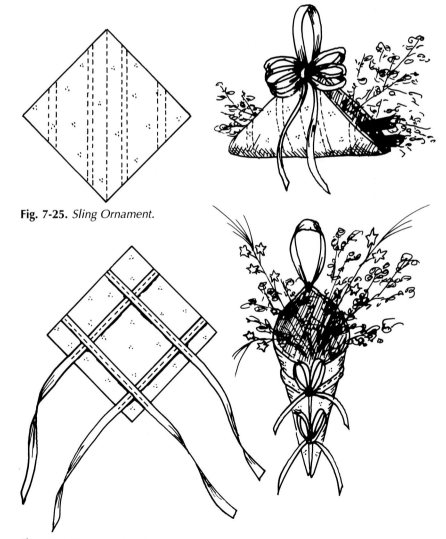

Fig. 7-25. *Sling Ornament.*

Fig. 7-26. *Cornucopia Ornament.*

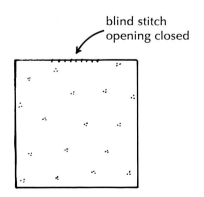

blind stitch
opening closed

Fig. 7-24. The basic 4″ block for the *Cornucopia* and *Sling Ornaments.*

3. To make the sling, first quilt the 4″ unit. Next take two opposite corners of the square and sew them together at the points to make the sling. Sew a loop of ribbon to hang

the ornament and add a decorative bow. It is now ready to fill (Fig. 7-25).

4. To make the cornucopia, stitch four 8″-long strips of ⅛″ ribbon to

the square piece (Fig. 7-26). To make the cornucopia shape, tie the loose ribbons together as shown in the diagram. Attach a loop to hang the ornament.

Star Ornament

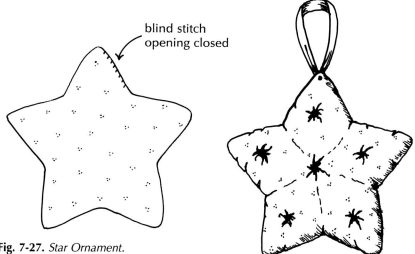

blind stitch
opening closed

Fig. 7-27. *Star Ornament.*

1. The stars can be any size you want. Several star sizes have been provided in the template section to be used for this project or as quilt-ing templates for other projects. Cut out two star pieces of the same size for each ornament. The two pieces can be cut from the same fabric or two different fabrics.

2. With right sides together, sew the two star pieces, leaving an opening large enough so that it can be turned inside out.

3. Stuff the star with fiberfill and blind stitch the opening closed. Do some tufted quilting by catching just enough fabric with your sewing needle to hold the tuft and then re-turning to the back of the star. Do this a few times in each tuft to make it secure. Make a small knot to finish it. A tuft in the center and in each of the points is shown in (Fig. 7-27).

4. Sew a ribbon loop to one of the points of the star and hang it on the tree.

Your tree can be beautifully decorated with these quilted ornaments. The *Cor-nucopia* and *Sling Ornaments* are made from 4″ squares of fabric and can be filled with anything that will fit.

Christmas Stocking

Stockings "hung by the chimney with care" is one of the strongest images of Christmas. Here's a simple stocking pattern for you to make and to enjoy for years to come.

Fabric Requirements

Fabric 1: ⅛ yard of gold lamé
Fabric 2: ½ yard of red moire taffeta
Fabric 3: ⅜ yard of green iridescent taffeta
Fabric 4: ⅛ yard of ivory satin
Fabric 5: ⅜ yard of unbleached muslin

Quantities Needed

1″ squares: cut 12 of Fabric 1, 48 of Fabric 2, 48 of Fabric 3
3″ squares: cut 12 of Fabric 4
Stocking lining: cut 2 from Fabric 2
Stocking back: cut 1 from Fabric 3

1. Prewash and dry the fabrics, then iron flat. Place the templates on each color of fabric, mark the patterns, and cut out.

2. Begin by sewing the 1″ squares together to create a nine-patch block, which is simply a block of three squares across and three squares down. The first row should be pieced as follows: one 1″ square of Fabric 3 stitched to one 1″ square of Fabric 2 and then stitched to one 1″ square of Fabric 3. Press all seams flat. The next row in your nine-patch should be a square of Fabric 2, a square of Fabric 1, then another square of Fabric 2. The last row is the same as the first. Pin the rows at the seam intersections and then stitch the first row to the second and then add the third. Continue until you have made 12 nine-patch blocks (Fig. 7-28).

3. Sew each nine-patch block to a 3″ square of Fabric 4. Press the seams flat. Sew the two pairs together, with the nine-patch and solid squares alternating, to make six rows of blocks.

Fig. 7-28. Nine-patch and solid squares used in the *Christmas Stocking*.

You can create several different patterns for stockings and still use the same fabrics so that they will work together. Here a nine-patch stocking project is shown with one that was strip pieced.

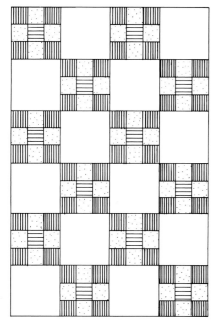

Fig. 7-29. Piecing diagram for stocking quilt block.

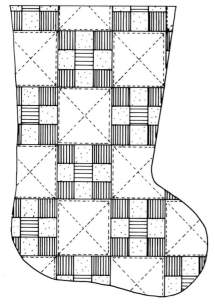

Fig. 7-30. Pieced stocking front.

4. Sew the rows together so that the blocks alternate like a checkerboard. Press all the seams flat. You now have a rectangular piece approximately 12″ × 18″ (Fig. 7-29).

5. Quilt the rectangle as desired. Use Fabric 5, which can be an inex-

pensive muslin, as a backing fabric because this won't show on the finished stocking.

6. Once you have completed quilting the rectangle use the template for the stocking to cut out the stocking front (Fig. 7-30). Cut out the linings and back of the stocking using the same template. For the lining, fold the fabric, with right sides together, and cut the two pieces out at the same time. Make sure when you are cutting out the backing fabric that you are cutting it the proper direction. The right side of the fabric should be the reverse of the right side of the stocking front.

7. Lay the right side of one lining piece on the right side of the stocking front, making sure they align. Now stitch across the top of the stocking. Do the same with the other lining piece and the back of the stocking.

8. Match the right sides of the lining and the right sides of the front and back, and pin (Fig. 7-31). Make a loop from ribbon for the hanger. It should be pinned in place between the layers at the back and top of the stocking. The loop should be under the layers with the loose ends hanging out of the edge.

9. Start sewing at the bottom of the stocking lining and sew around the entire stocking stopping about 2½″ before your starting point. Take the pins out and turn the stocking inside out through the opening you have left. Turn the seam under at the opening and machine stitch near the edge to close the hole.

10. Stuff the lining into the stocking and press the stocking (Fig. 7-32). It is now ready to hang by the fireplace.

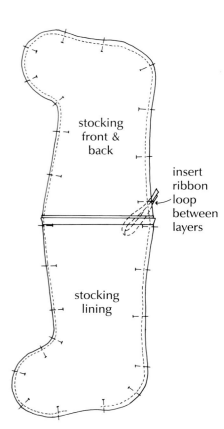

Fig. 7-31. Layout for sewing the lining and stocking together.

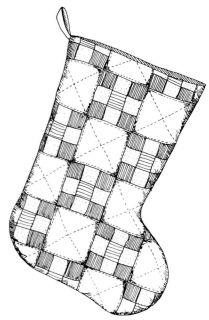

Fig. 7-32. Finished *Christmas Stocking*.

CHAPTER EIGHT

Quilts Just for Fun!

Game Board

(Finished dimensions: 24" square.)

This project is a good one to make for children. The Game Board can be easily packed in a suitcase and taken along on vacations, or it can be brought along to family gatherings so that all can enjoy a friendly game of checkers.

Wooden checkers can be purchased at your local crafts store and paint or stain them in colors that complement your Game Board. For a chess game, paint symbols on the back side of the checkers to represent chess pieces.

Note: This small quilt presents the perfect opportunity to utilize scrap fabrics, with both Fabric 1 and Fabric 2 using less than ¼ yard. The quilt pictured has a solid piece of fabric as backing, but a pieced back using larger scraps would work as well.

Fabric Requirements

Fabric 1: ¼ yard of white
Fabric 2: ¼ yard of black
Fabric 3: 1 yard of teal and black print

Quantities Needed

Center section:
2" squares: cut 32 of Fabric 1, 32 of Fabric 2
4" solid square: cut 4 of Fabric 2
4" quarter triangle: cut 32 of Fabric 3, 32 of Fabric 1
Backing: cut from Fabric 3
Binding: make 3 yards of binding from Fabric 3

1. Prewash and dry all fabrics, then iron flat. Place the templates on the fabrics and mark pattern on each color to be used. Cut out the required number of squares and triangles.

2. To make the checkerboard, piece by joining one 2" square of Fabric 1 and one 2" square of Fabric 2, with right sides together, to create pairs. Stitch together, using ¼" seam allowance. Repeat with the remaining 2" square pieces. Next, join two pairs together, alternating the colors, to make a set of four rectangles. Stitch together two sets of four into a strip of eight, maintaining alternating colors along the length of the strip. Press all the seam allowances in one direction for all eight strips. Sew two strips of eight together, matching alternating color squares. Align the seams with pins. Eight strips will become four larger strips. Complete piecing the check-

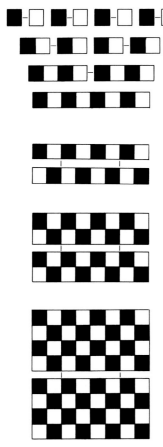

Fig. 8-1. Piecing diagram for the checkerboard.

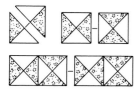

Fig. 8-2. Piecing diagram for border.

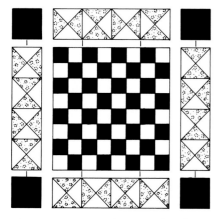

Fig. 8-3. Piecing diagram for *Game Board.*

The colors and fabrics used in the *Game Board* give it a contemporary feel.

erboard by combining four strips into two, then two into one. Press all the new seam allowances in the same direction. Set aside the checkerboard (Fig. 8-1).

3. Stitch, with right sides together, pairs of 4″ quarter triangles along the short sides, using one of Fabric 1 and one of Fabric 3. This will create 32 larger triangle halves. Press the seam allowances toward the darker side and match the seam on one triangle half to another triangle half, alternating colors. Stitch together on the long edge to make 4″ pieced squares, pressing the seam allowances to one side (Fig. 8-2). Sew four pieced squares together to make one section of border, pressing all seam allowances. Repeat with the remaining pieced squares, to make a total of four sections of border. Join two 4″ solid squares to one border section, pressing seam allowances, and repeat with second border section. Attach the other two border sections to the top and bottom of the checkerboard, matching all seams. Stitch a solid square/pieced square border section to one side of the quilt, matching the seams. Complete the quilt top by attaching the last solid square/pieced square border section to the opposite side of the quilt and stitch (Fig. 8-3). Press the seam allowances flat.

4. Quilt and bind as desired (Fig. 8-4). Refer to Chapter Three, Quilting Basics.

Fig. 8-4. Finished *Game Board.*

Naptime Clown Quilt and Pillow

This quilt and pillow are a lot of fun to make and to give as a gift. The quilt can be used not only as a blanket, but also as a kind of "costume" for the child to hold in front of himself. The pillow was designed to make the clown complete.

Other characters and animals can be designed in the same manner. Just let your imagination run wild or let your child help design his or her favorite.

Note: With this quilt you will need to make your own templates to size. Draw the needed shapes onto lightweight cardboard. Use the diagrams in Fig. 8-5 for the measurements of template pieces. Because buttons are used, this quilt is not recommended for very small children, who might pull the buttons loose and swallow them.

Quilt (Finished dimensions: 36″ × 48″.)

Fabric Requirements

Fabric 1: 1 yard of light yellow solid
Fabric 2: 1 yard of medium yellow solid
Fabric 3: 1 yard of dark yellow solid
Fabric 4: 1 yard of orange solid
Fabric 5: 1 yard of purple solid
Fabric 6: 1 yard of multicolored polka dot
Fabric 7: 1 yard of pale pink solid
Fabric 8: 3 yards of green solid
Fabric 9: 3 yards of red polka dot
Backing: cut from Fabric 9
Binding: make 5 yards of binding from Fabric 8
Grosgrain ribbon: 3 yards of white

1. Prewash and dry the fabrics, then iron flat.

2. Cut out all of the fabric pieces (Fig. 8-5) according to the directions in Chapter Three, Quilting Basics, on appliqué. One template can be used for both pieces A and B—just reverse the template to cut piece A. The same holds true for pieces E and C, D and F, G and H, J and K, and L and I. Add a ¼″ seam allowance to all pattern pieces. Templates for D/F and the pocket can be found at the back of the book.

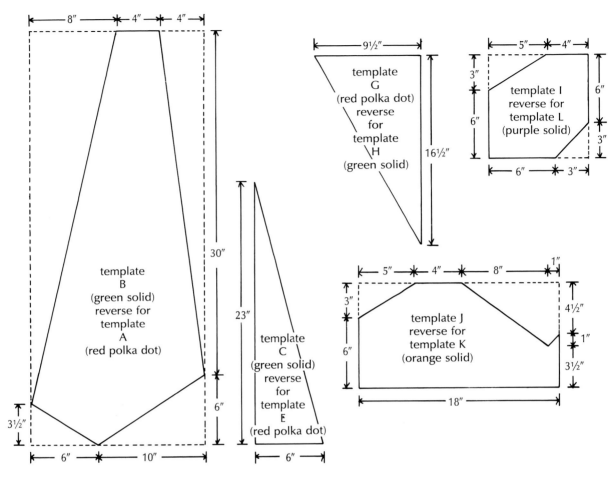

Fig. 8-5. Diagram for creating templates for *Naptime Clown Quilt.*

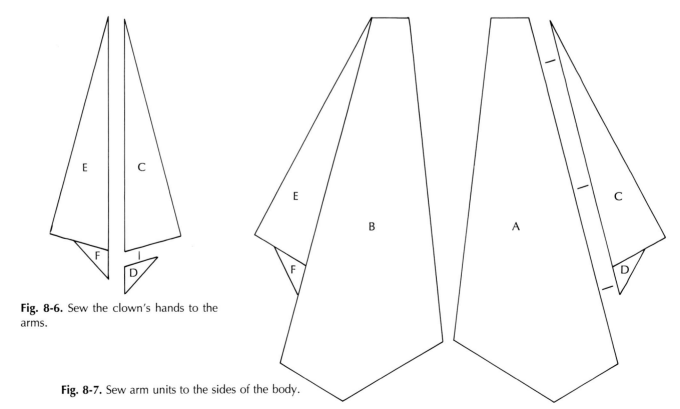

Fig. 8-6. Sew the clown's hands to the arms.

Fig. 8-7. Sew arm units to the sides of the body.

3. Sew hands (D and F) to arms (E and C) as shown in the piecing diagram (Fig. 8-6). Press the seam toward the arms. Then sew the arms to the body sections (A and B) (Fig. 8-7). Position the narrow point of the arms to the narrow end of the body sections, and sew. Press seams toward the body section. Press the remaining edges over ¼" to prepare pieces for appliquéing later. Set these pieces aside.

4. Sew the legs (G and H) together as shown (Fig. 8-8). Press angled sides under ¼" so that they can be appliquéd later. Set the legs aside.

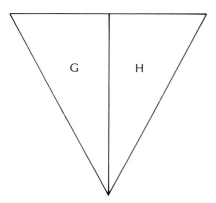

Fig. 8-8. Sew the two legs together.

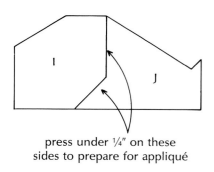

press under ¼" on these sides to prepare for appliqué

Fig. 8-9. Sew toe to shoe.

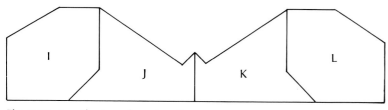

Fig. 8-10. Sew the two shoes together.

5. To make the shoes, prepare pieces I and L so that they can be appliquéd to pieces J and K. This is done by pressing under ¼" of fabric on the two sides as shown in Fig. 8-9. After pressing, place piece I over piece J and blind stitch the two prepared sides of piece I to piece J. Follow the same procedure for pieces K and L.

6. Sew the two shoe units together in the middle (Fig. 8-10). Press the top sides of the shoes under ¼" so that they can be appliquéd later. Set the shoes aside.

7. Cut out six pieces of the background fabrics, 16½" × 18½" (¼" seam allowance *included*). The quilt in the photograph has a background of three shades of yellow, but you can use whatever fabric combinations you wish. Assemble pieces as shown in Fig. 8-11. This layout of the background fabrics will help with the positioning of the appliqué pieces later.

8. Lay the leg pieces onto the background fabric first. Align the top of the legs with the first horizontal seam from the bottom and align the middle seam of the legs with the middle seam of the background. Pin the legs into place. Position the shoes at the bottom of the quilt. Align the bottom of the shoes with the bottom of the background. Pin the shoes in place. Position the body sides on the background by aligning the top left corner of the right side with the top middle seam

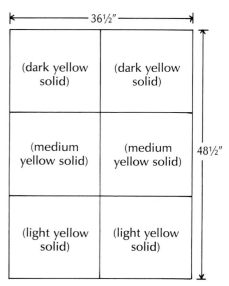

Fig. 8-11. Piecing diagram for background.

of the background. Align the top right corner of the left side to the middle seam of the background. The left side should overlap the right side as shown in the piecing diagram (Fig. 8-12). Adjust the body until the pieces align as shown. Pin the body sections in place.

9. Blind stitch around all exposed edges to appliqué to the background. Set aside.

10. Prepare the pocket by pressing all edges under ¼". Stitch along the top edge to hold under the seam allowance. Set the pocket aside.

11. Make the handkerchief for the pocket by cutting two 12½" squares of multicolored polka dot fabric. Lay the right sides of the fabric together and stitch, using ¼" seam all around, leaving a 2" opening. Turn inside out and press flat. Blind stitch the opening closed.

12. Decide where to place the pocket. Before pinning the pocket in place, position the handkerchief and stitch across the bottom so that

cut for collar

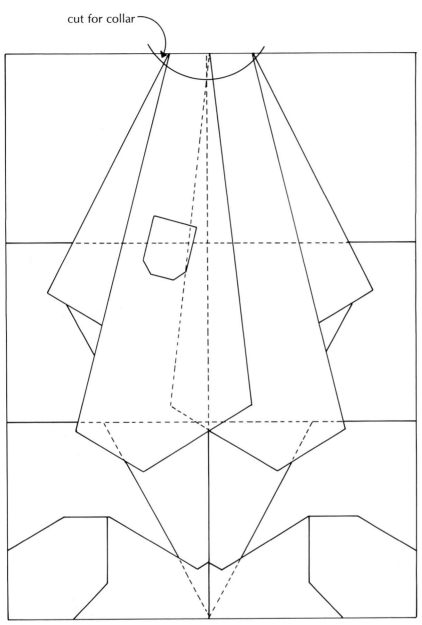

Fig. 8-12. Placement of pieces on the background.

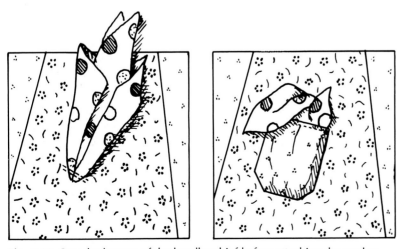

Fig. 8-13. Sew the bottom of the handkerchief before attaching the pocket.

it will stay in place (Fig. 8-13). Pin the pocket over the handkerchief and blind stitch around three sides leaving the top edge open. The handkerchief will stick out of the top of the pocket. Tack the top of the handkerchief to the quilt to keep it from drooping. To do this, make a few stitches through the handkerchief and the rest of the layers of the quilt top.

13. Sew the shoe laces, which are made from two 48″-long pieces of ¾″ grosgrain ribbon. Fold the two lengths in half and pin the doubled ribbon in place. Blind stitch on both sides of the ribbon and across the section where they will tie.

14. Sew the buttons firmly into place on the clown's outfit (1½″ buttons were used on the example pictured).

15. Quilt as desired. Refer to Chapter Three, Quilting Basics.

16. Before binding the quilt, make the ruffle. Cut out a piece of multicolored polka dot fabric 16½″ × 24½″. Fold the fabric in half lengthwise, with right sides together, to create a piece that is 8¼″ × 24½″. Sew a ¼″ seam on both ends of the fabric. Turn the fabric right side out and press. With a sewing machine on the widest stitch setting, stitch two rows of stitches on the unsewn 24″ side, with one row ⅛″ from the edge and the other ¼″, leaving long threads hanging from both ends. Separate the threads and pull one set of threads until the fabric starts to ruffle. Continue pulling the threads until the fabric measures 12″ (Fig. 8-14).

17. Using a dinner plate, draw a partial circle at the top center of the quilt. This is for placement of the collar. Cut out this area and position the ruffled collar at its edge,

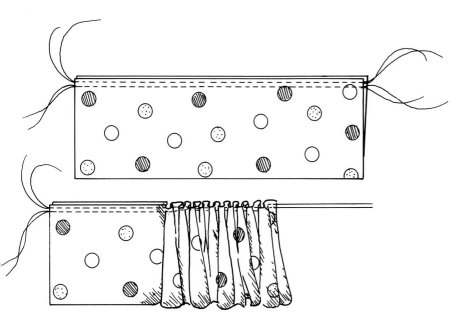

Fig. 8-14. Creating the ruffle.

leaving at least ½″ of space from the quilt top edges to the curved beginnings of the collar. Hand baste the collar into place. Bind the quilt, including around the inside edges of the collar (Fig. 8-15).

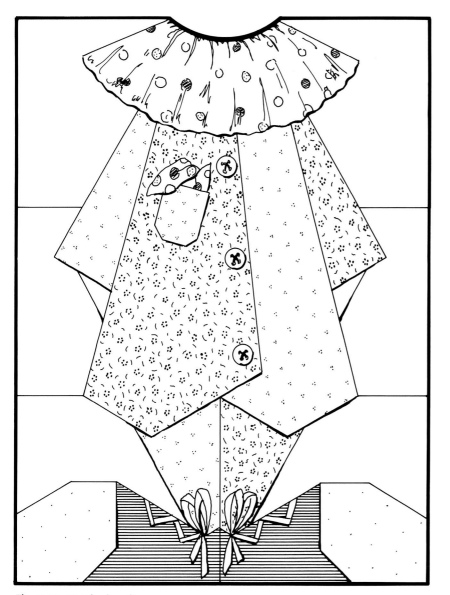

Fig. 8-15. Finished quilt.

Pillow

Fabric Requirements

The yardages given for the Naptime Clown Quilt will cover the fabrics needed for the pillow. All other pieces can be made out of scrap fabric.

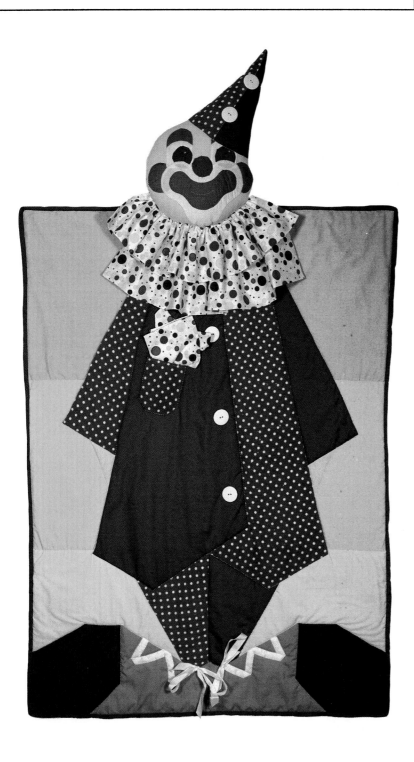

1. Iron flat any pieces of scrap fabric.

2. Using the templates in the back of this book, create and prepare appliqués as instructed in Chapter Three, Quilting Basics.

3. The head is made from a 12½″ round circle. Sew the two hat pieces together in the middle and then press the bottom curved edge under ¼″ (Fig. 8-16). Set the hat aside. Next, lay out all the appliqué pieces in position on the face, and pin in place (Fig. 8-17). Blind stitch around the exposed edges to appliqué the pieces in place. When finished appliquéing the facial features, place the hat where desired and blind stitch the bottom of the hat in place. Quilt the head section as desired.

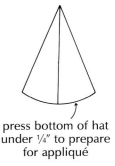

press bottom of hat
under ¼″ to prepare
for appliqué

Fig. 8-16. Sew the hat pieces together.

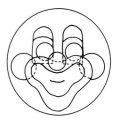

Fig. 8-17. Placement of appliqué pieces on the clown's face.

The three-dimensional clown quilt is a favorite of children. The clown's head is a pillow which can be detached when your child wants to use the quilt to play with. The laces can be used to teach children how to tie their shoes.

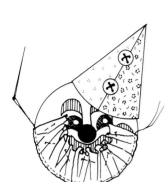

Fig. 8-18. Baste the ruffle to the edge of the clown's face and pin ruffle down to keep it out of the way when sewing the pillow top to the pillow back.

4. Next sew the buttons securely on the hat.

5. To create the pillow backing, turn the clown face right side down onto the right side of the backing fabric and trim around the edge of the clown face. Lay these pieces aside.

6. Create the clown pillow ruffle by cutting a 10½″ × 24½″ piece of fabric. Follow the instructions for making the ruffle, which can be found in the Naptime Clown Quilt instructions. Hand baste and pin the ruffle to the clown face (Fig. 8-18). Lay the clown face with the ruffle face up. Lay the backing fabric right side down and pin in place. Stitch a ¼″ seam around the pillow shape leaving a 2″ opening at the

Fig. 8-19. Finished pillow.

ruffle. Turn the pillow inside out. Stuff the pillow with fiberfill, and blind stitch the opening closed (Fig. 8-19).

Pencil Wall Quilt

(Finished dimensions: 36″ square.)

This is a fun project for a child's bedroom or playroom. You can make one pencil or 101 pencils connected together. The fabric amounts given are for eight pencils of the same color. If you want to make the pencils different colors, you will need only scraps of three values of each color that are the length of the pencil shaft.

This quilt is interesting because of the different value of the colors and the irregular edges.

Fabric Requirements

Fabric 1: 2½ yards of light yellow
Fabric 2: ½ yard of medium yellow
Fabric 3: ½ yard of dark yellow
Fabric 4: ¼ yard of light mauve
Fabric 5: ¼ yard of medium mauve
Fabric 6: ¼ yard of dark mauve

Fabric 7: ¼ yard of light gray
Fabric 8: ¼ yard of medium gray
Fabric 9: ¼ yard of dark gray
Fabric 10: ¼ yard of light brown
Fabric 11: ¼ yard of medium brown
Fabric 12: ¼ yard of dark brown

Quantities Needed

Pencil shaft: cut 8 from Fabric 1, 2″ × 28″ strips; cut 8 from Fabric 2, 2″ × 28″ strips; cut 8 from Fabric 3, 2″ × 28″ strips
Pencil eraser: cut 8 from Fabric 4, 2″ × 5″ strips; cut 8 from Fabric 5, 2″ × 5″ strips; cut 8 from Fabric 6, 2″ × 5″ strips
Metal shanks: cut 8 from Fabric 7, 1½″ × 5″ strips; cut 8 from Fabric 8, 3″ × 5″ strips; cut 8 from Fabric 9, 1½″ × 5″ strips
Pencil lead: cut 8 from Fabric 9

Pencil points: cut 8 from Fabric 10, 8 from Fabric 11, 8 from Fabric 12
Backing: cut from Fabric 1
Binding: cut from Fabric 1

1. Prewash and dry the fabrics, then press flat. Cut out the strips needed to complete the quilt. Also, using the templates, cut out the pieces needed for the pencil lead and pencil point.

2. Sew the pencil shaft strips, long sides together, in groups of three from lightest to darkest. Repeat with the eraser, metal shank, and pencil point pieces (Fig. 8-20A). Using the cutting templates, cut the arches for the eraser, shank, and point pieces. The cut dimension on the side of the eraser and metal shank sections should be 3½″ (Fig. 8-20B).

3. Pin and sew erasers to the metal shanks. Begin by pinning in the middle of each and working toward the outside. Stitch in place, using a ¼″ seam, easing the curves to fit, and press open. Next, sew the pencil shaft to the eraser/shank section, also beginning in the center, and easing curves to fit. Set aside the pencil shaft section.

4. Align the pencil lead and pencil point and sew across. The lead piece should extend over the point approximately ¼″. Cut off the excess pencil point fabric and press all seams flat. Next, press the top edges of the pencil points under, with wrong sides together, to prepare them to be appliquéd to the pencil shaft. To appliqué, position the left corner of the point 25″ from the spot where the metal shank meets with the pencil shaft (Fig. 8-20C).

5. Blind stitch the point to the rest of the pencil and trim excess yellow fabric from behind the pencil point (Fig. 8-20D). Repeat with the remaining pencils. Pin, with right sides together, the eight pencils,

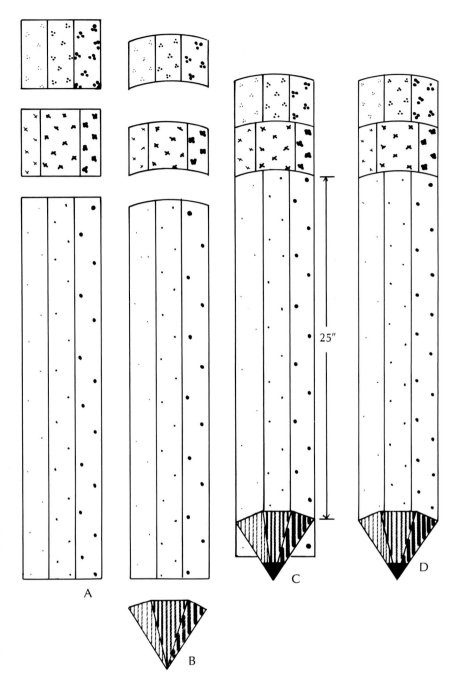

Fig. 8-20. Piecing diagram for the pencils.

matching them along the long edges.

6. Place on a flat surface a piece of backing fabric flat, wrong side up, and center a piece of batting on top. Center the pencil quilt top over the backing/batting and baste together, stitching through all the layers. Quilt as desired. Trim away excess fabric, and bind the quilt. Stitch the binding by hand, using a blind stitch (Fig. 8-21).

The *Pencil Wall Quilt* can be easily adapted to any color combination. Here yellow was used to mimic standard No. 2 pencils. The use of different values of color is what makes this quilt successful, and the irregular edge adds to its interest.

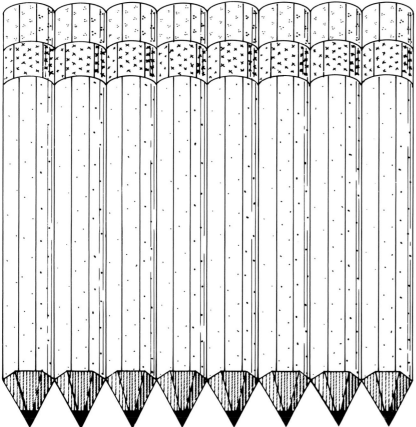

Fig. 8-21. Finished *Pencil Wall Quilt*.

Bibliography

Albers, Joseph. *Interaction of Color.* New Haven, CT: Yale University Press, 1963.

Bacon, Lenice Ingram. *American Patchwork Quilts.* New York: Bonanza Books, 1980.

Beyer, Jinny. *Jinny Beyer's Color Confidence for Quilters.* Gualala, CA: The Quilt Digest Press, 1992.

Cairns, Pat. *Contemporary Quilting Techniques — A Modular Approach.* Radnor, PA: Chilton Book Company, 1991.

Dee, Anne Patterson. *Quilter's Sourcebook.* Radnor, PA: Wallace-Homestead Book Company, 1987.

Dittman, Margaret. *The Fabric Lover's Scrapbook.* Radnor, PA: Chilton Book Company, 1988.

_____ . *Fourteen Easy Baby Quilts.* Radnor, PA: Chilton Book Company, 1991.

Eaton, Kathleen. *Super Simple Quilts.* Radnor, PA: Chilton Book Company, 1992.

Echols, Margit. *Classic Patchwork and Quilting.* New York: Sedgewood Press, 1990.

Frager, Dorothy. *The Quilting Primer.* Radnor, PA: Chilton Book Company, 1974.

Hall, Jane, and Dixie Haywood. *Precision Pieced Quilts Using the Foundation Method.* Radnor, PA: Chilton Book Company, 1992.

Hatch, Sandra L., and Anne Boyce. *Putting on The Glitz — Unusual Fabrics and Threads for Quilting and Sewing.* Radnor, PA: Chilton Book Company, 1991.

Holstein, Jonathan. *American Pieced Quilts.* New York: Viking Press, 1972.

_____ . *The Pieced Quilt: An American Tradition.* Boston: Little, Brown & Co., 1973.

Horton, Roberta. *An Amish Adventure: A Workbook for Color in Quilts.* Lafayette, CA: C & T Publishing, 1983.

Ickis, Marguerite. *The Standard Book of Quiltmaking and Collecting.* New York: Dover Publications, 1959.

Itten, Johannes. *The Elements of Color — A Treatise on the Color System of Johannes Itten.* Edited by Ernst Van Hagen. New York: Van Nostrand Reinhold Company, 1970.

Jackman, Dianne R., and Mary K. Dixon. *The Guide to Textiles for Interior Designers.* Winnepeg: Peguis Publishers, Ltd., 1983.

James, Michael. *The Quiltmaker's Handbook: A Guide to Design and Construction.* Englewood Cliffs, NJ: Prentice-Hall, 1978.

Johnson, Frances. *Collecting Antique Linens, Lace and Needlework.* Radnor, PA: Chilton Book Company, 1991.

Leman, Bonnie. *Quick and Easy Quilting.* Wheatridge, CO: Moon Over the Mountain Publishing, 1972.

Nuckolls, James L. *Interior Lighting for Environmental Designers.* New York: John Wiley and Sons, 1976.

Orlofsk, Patsy and Myron. *Quilts in America.* New York: McGraw-Hill, 1974.

Packham, Jo, and Terrece Beesely. *Vanessa-Ann's Living with Quilts.* New York: Meredith Press, 1991.

Pellman, Rachel and Kenneth. *The World of Amish Quilts.* Intercourse, PA: Good Books, 1984.

Puentes, Nancy O'Bryant. *First Aid for Family Quilts.* Wheatridge, CO: Moon Over the Mountain Publishing, 1986.

Schaeffer, Claire B. *Claire Schaeffer's Fabric Sewing Guide.* Radnor, PA: Chilton Book Company, 1989.

Seward, Linda. *The Complete Book of Patchwork, Quilting and Appliqué.* New York: Prentice-Hall, 1987.

Sharpe, Deborah T. *The Psychology of Color and Design.* Chicago: Nelson Hall Publishers, 1974.

Sinema, Laurene. *Appliqué!, Appliqué!!, Appliqué!!!.* Gualala, CA: The Quilt Digest Press, 1992.

Soltow, Willow Ann. *Kid's Very Own Quilt Book.* Lombard, IL: Wallace-Homestead Book Company, 1986.

_____. *Quilting the World Over.* Radnor, PA: Chilton Book Company, 1991.

Stockton, James. *Designer's Guide to Color.* San Francisco: Chronicle Books, 1983.

_____. *Designer's Guide to Color 2.* San Francisco: Chronicle Books, 1984.

Time-Life Books, Inc. *Country Quilts.* Alexandria, VA: Time-Life Books, 1989.

von Goethe, Johann Wolfgang. *Theory of Colors.* Cambridge and London: MIT Press, 1970.

Wagner, Debra. *Teach Yourself Machine Piecing and Quilting.* Radnor, PA: Chilton Book Company, 1992.

Wentworth, Judy. *Quilts.* London: Studio Editions, Inc., 1989.

Templates

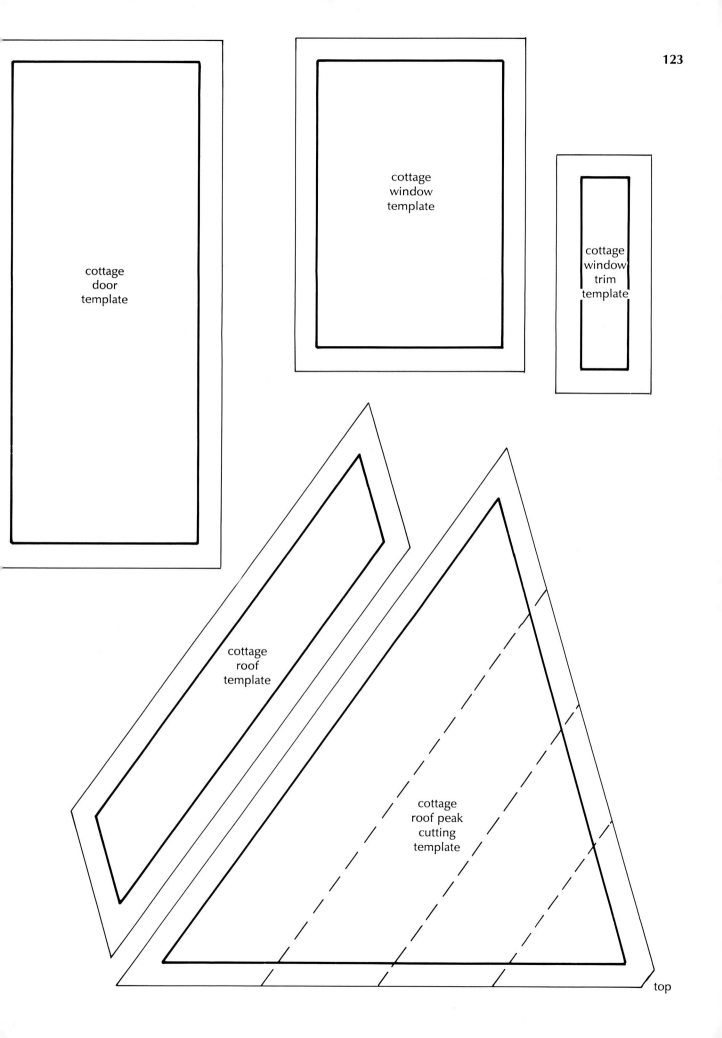

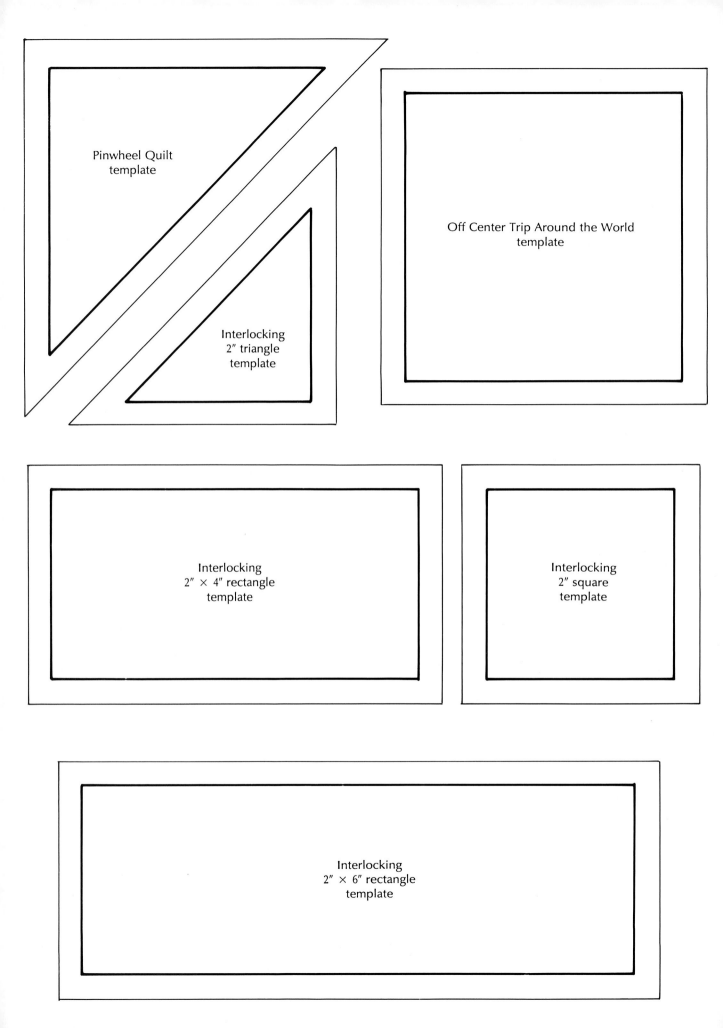

Pinwheel Quilt
template

Interlocking
2″ triangle
template

Off Center Trip Around the World
template

Interlocking
2″ × 4″ rectangle
template

Interlocking
2″ square
template

Interlocking
2″ × 6″ rectangle
template

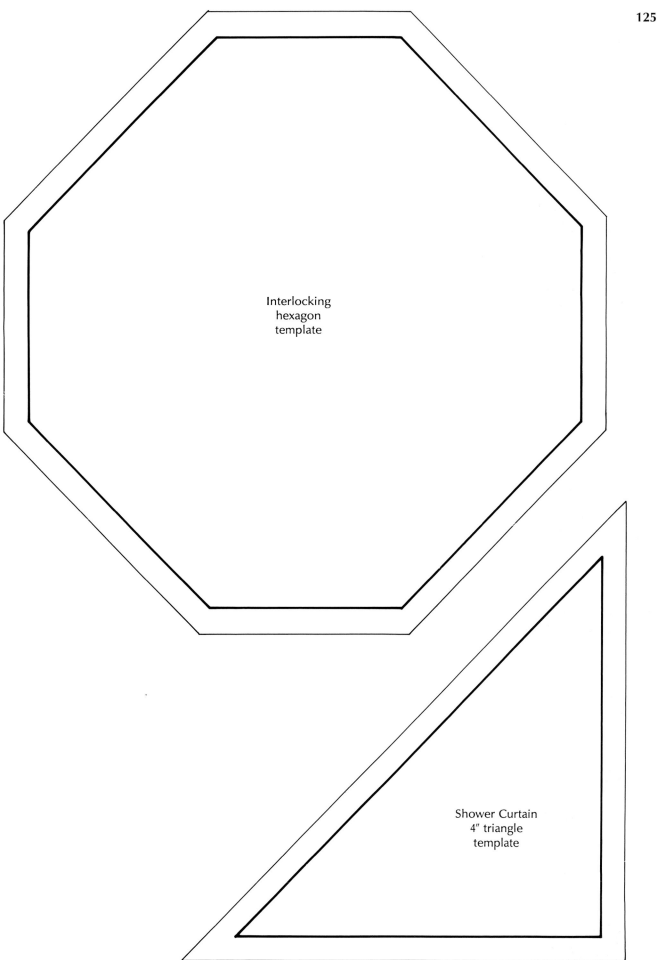

Interlocking
hexagon
template

Shower Curtain
4″ triangle
template

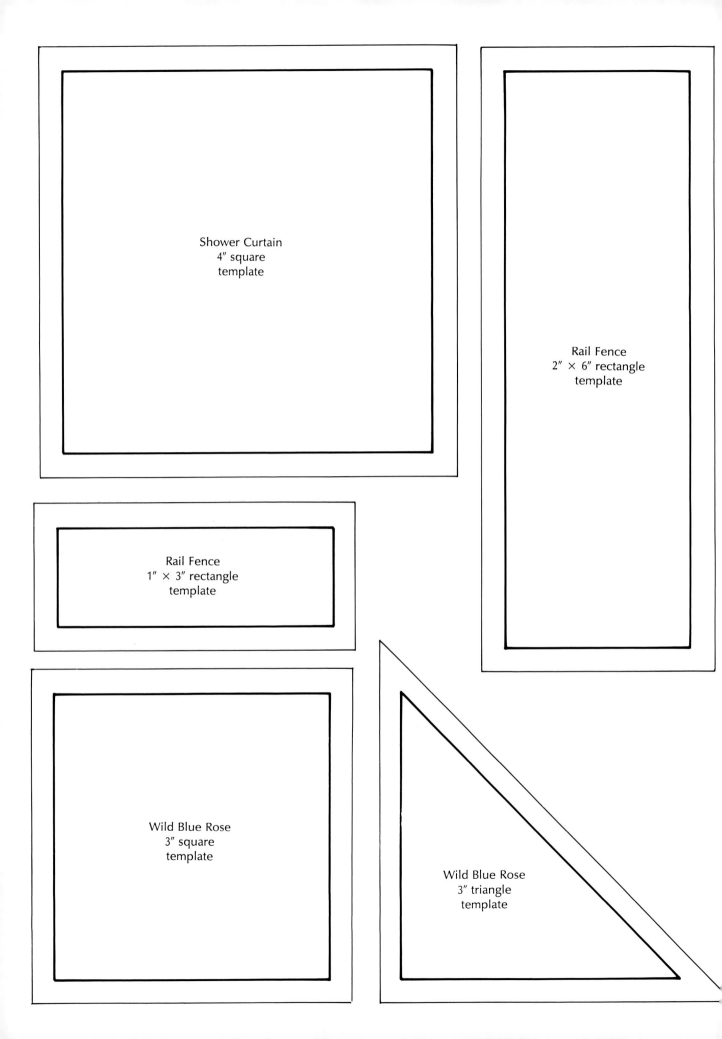

Shower Curtain
4″ square
template

Rail Fence
2″ × 6″ rectangle
template

Rail Fence
1″ × 3″ rectangle
template

Wild Blue Rose
3″ square
template

Wild Blue Rose
3″ triangle
template

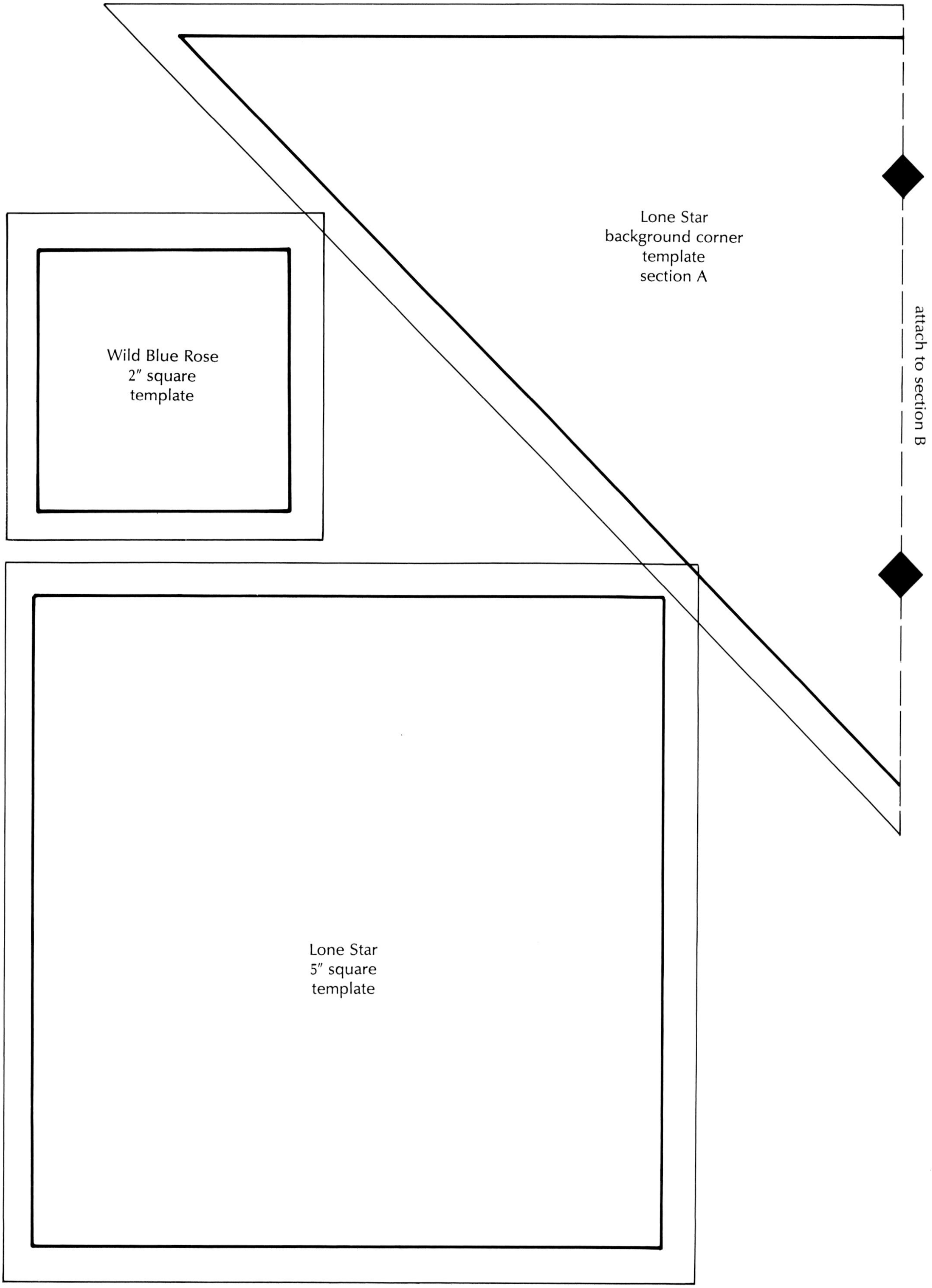

Lone Star
background corner
template
section A

Wild Blue Rose
2″ square
template

attach to section B

Lone Star
5″ square
template

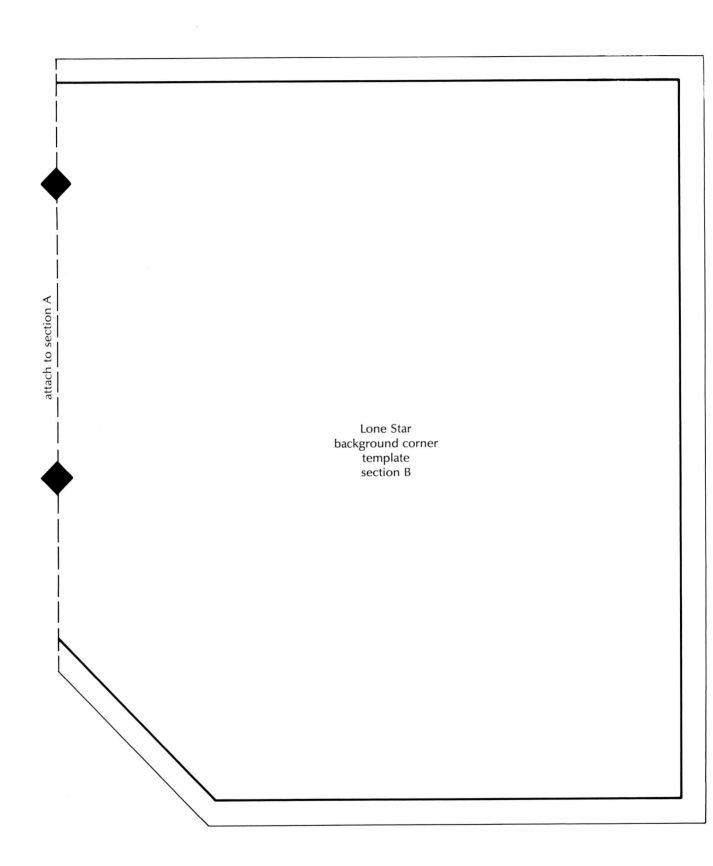

attach to section A

Lone Star
background corner
template
section B

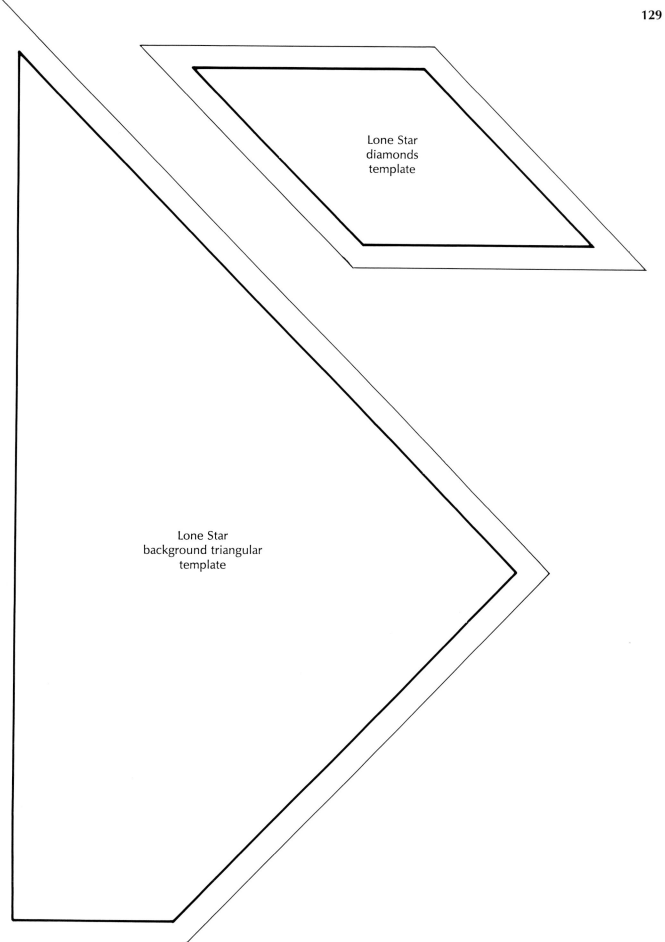

Lone Star
diamonds
template

Lone Star
background triangular
template

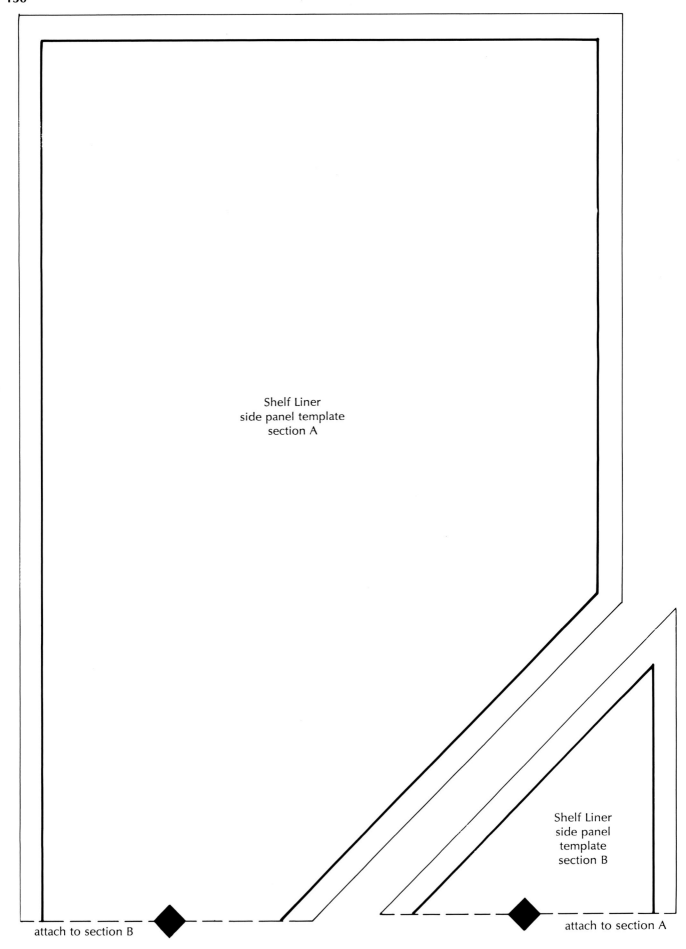

Shelf Liner
side panel template
section A

Shelf Liner
side panel
template
section B

attach to section B

attach to section A

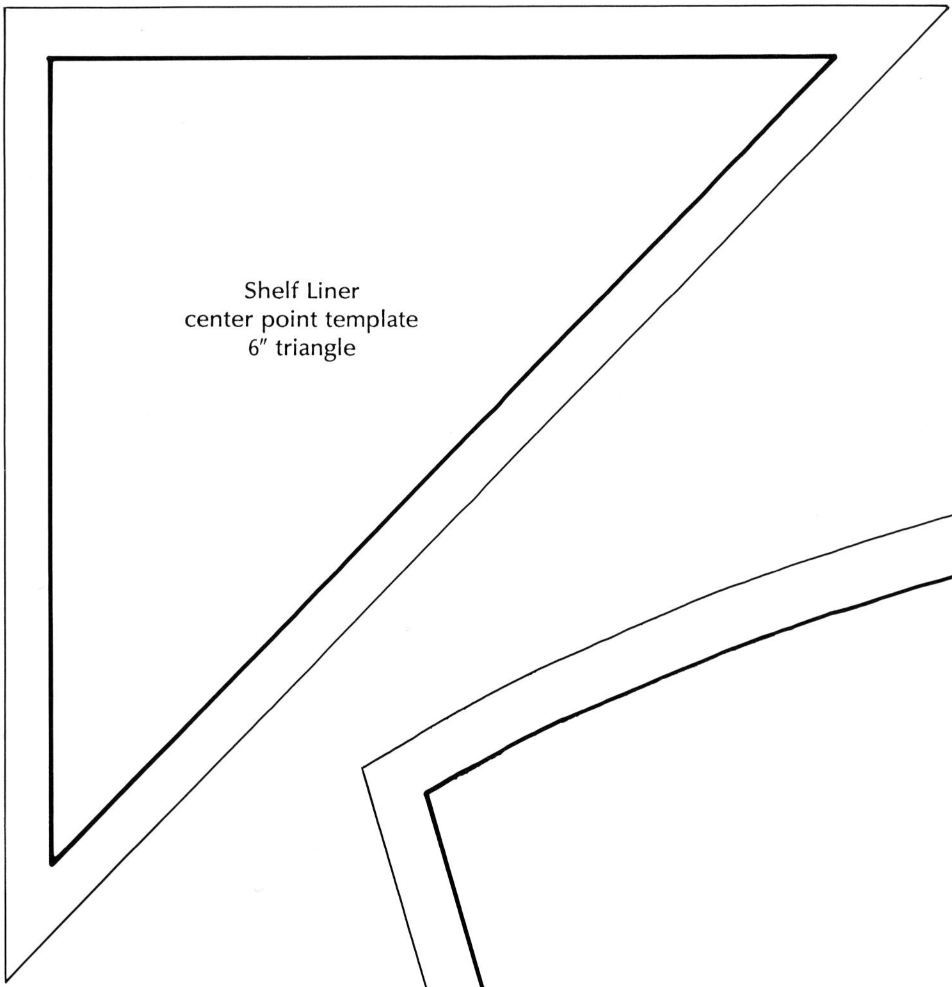

Shelf Liner
center point template
6″ triangle

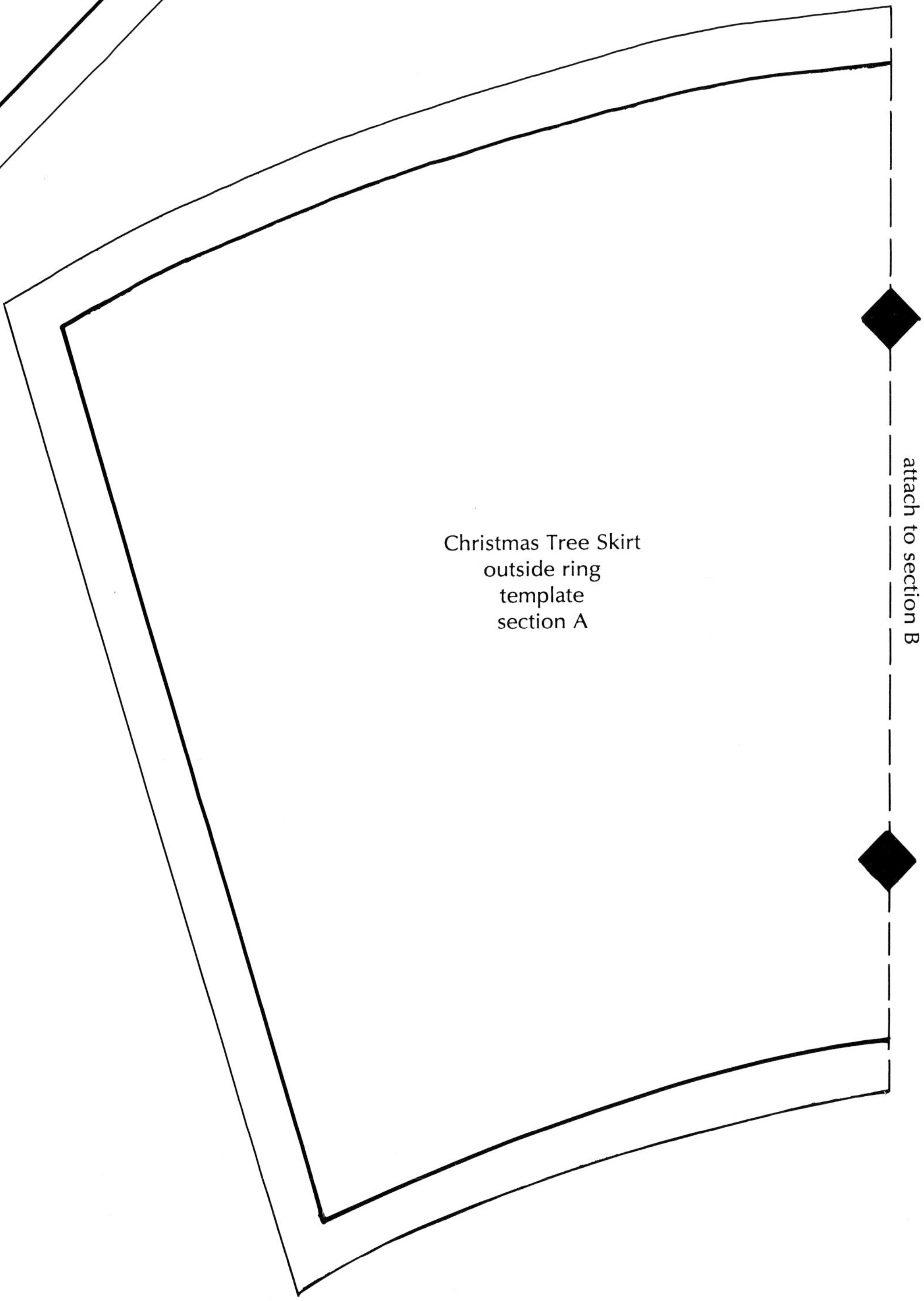

Christmas Tree Skirt
outside ring
template
section A

attach to section B

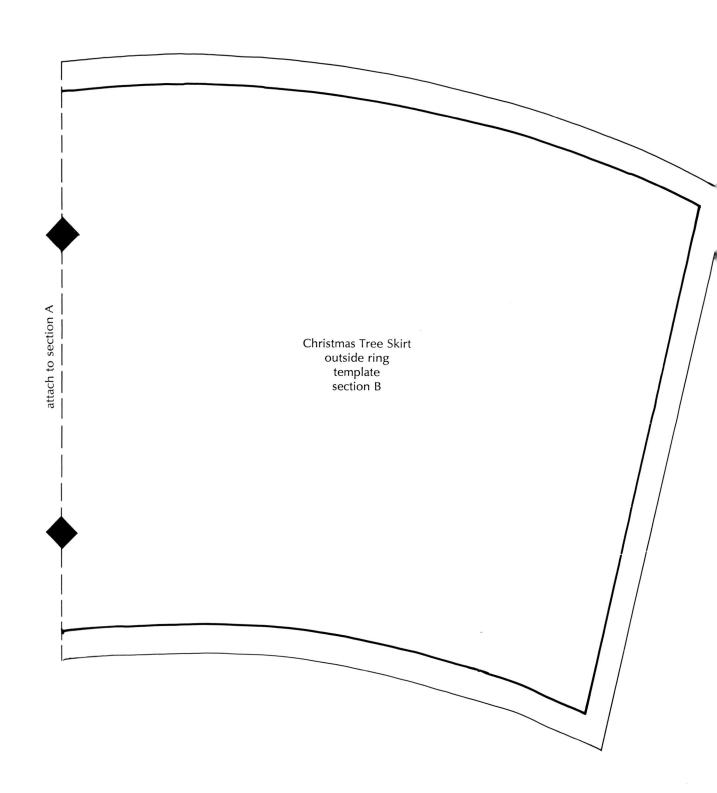

attach to section A

Christmas Tree Skirt
outside ring
template
section B

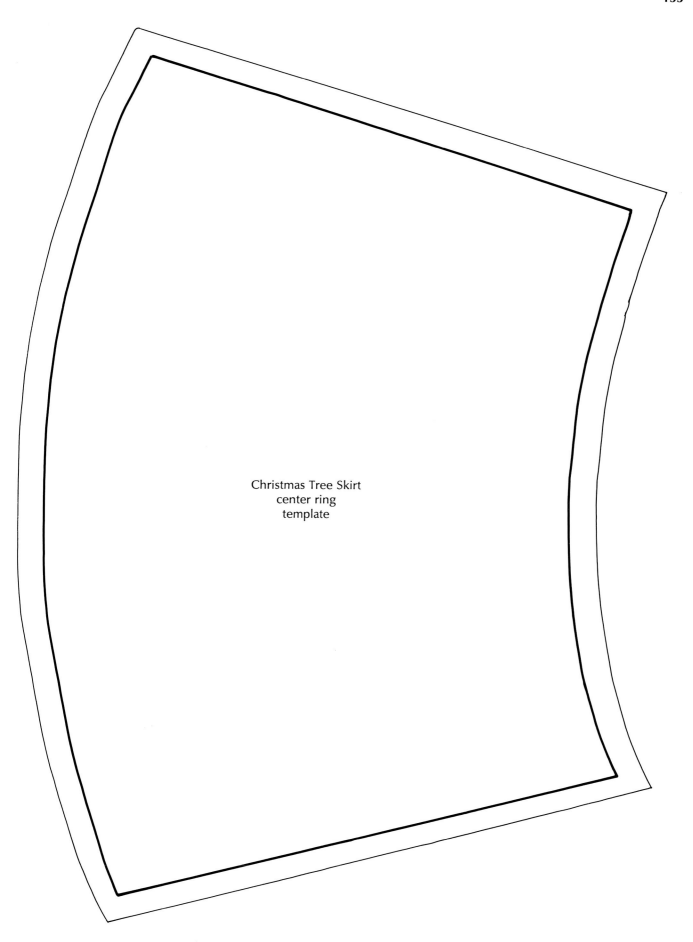

Christmas Tree Skirt
center ring
template

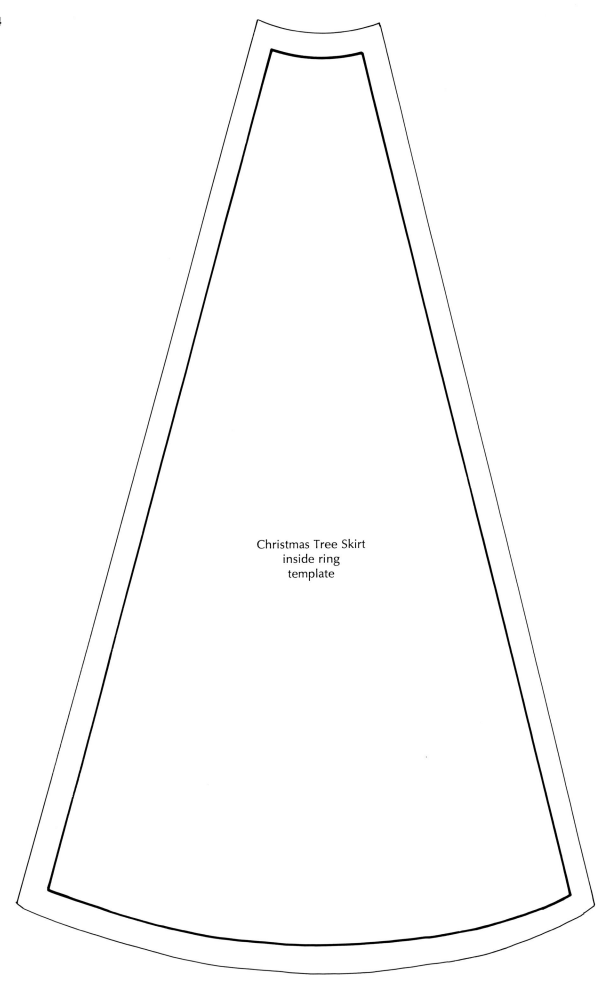

Christmas Tree Skirt
inside ring
template

Christmas Tree Ornaments
(Cornucopia and Sling)
4″ square
template

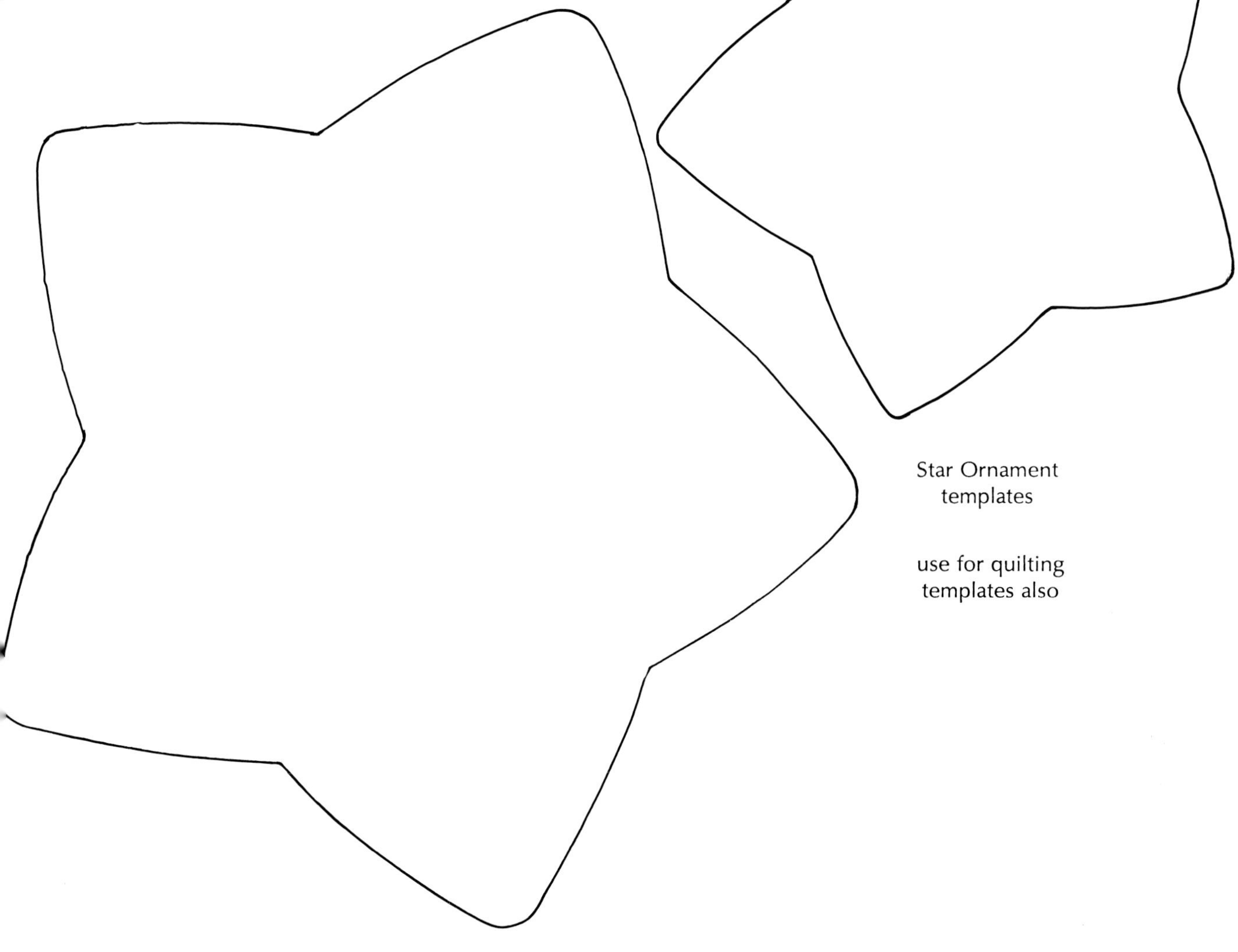

Star Ornament
templates

use for quilting
templates also

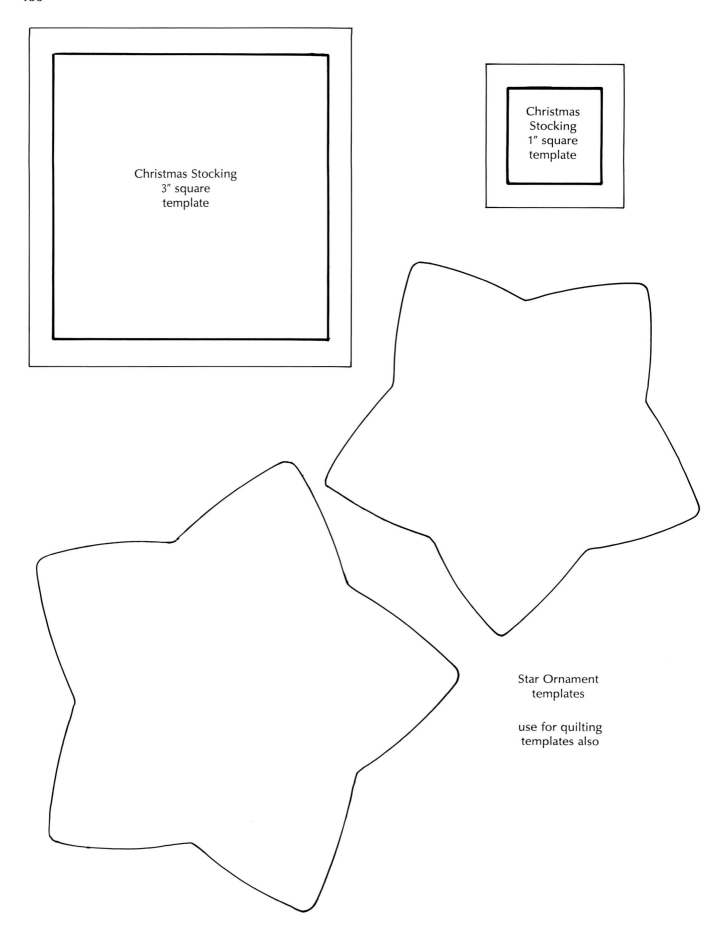

Christmas Stocking
3″ square
template

Christmas
Stocking
1″ square
template

Star Ornament
templates

use for quilting
templates also

Christmas Stocking Template (half size)

one square = one inch

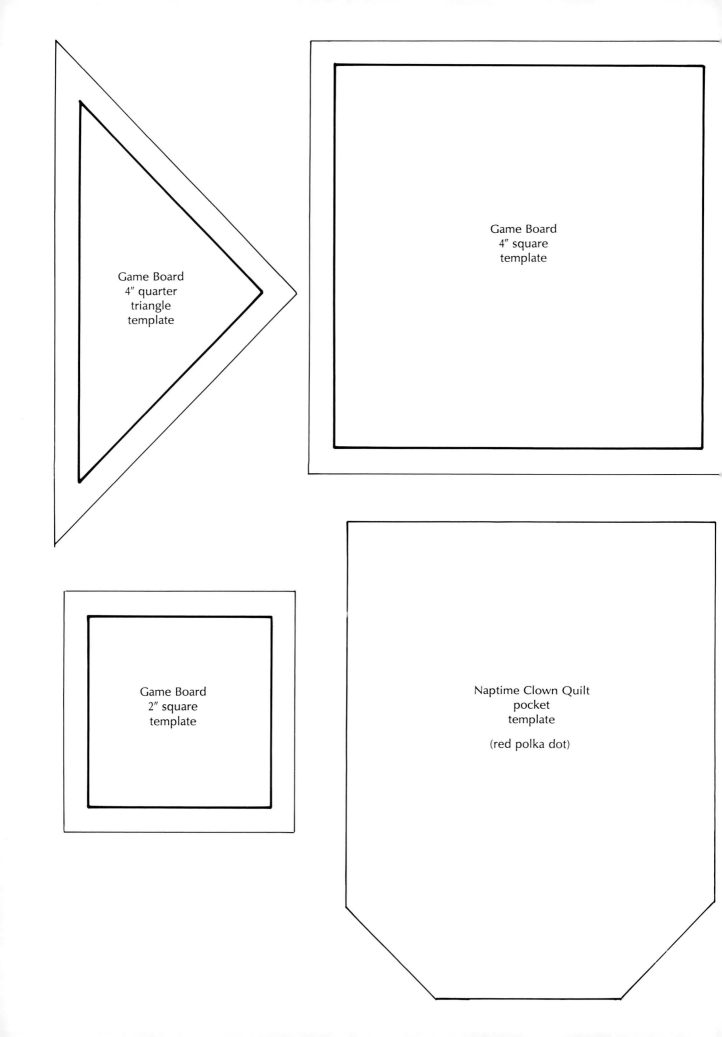

Game Board
4″ quarter
triangle
template

Game Board
4″ square
template

Game Board
2″ square
template

Naptime Clown Quilt
pocket
template

(red polka dot)

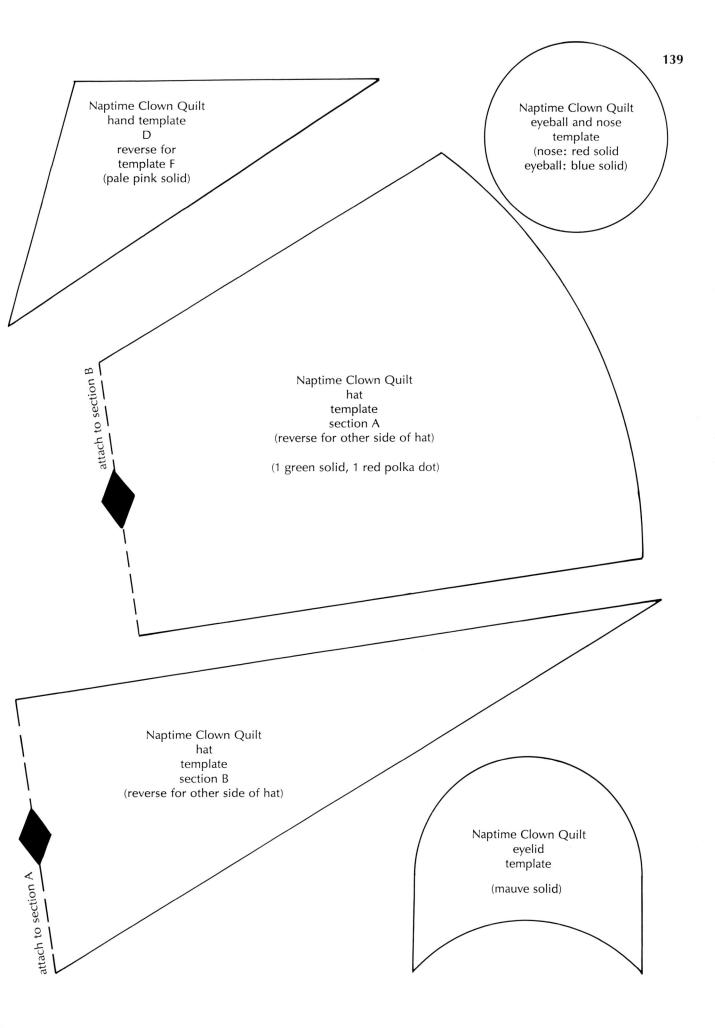

Naptime Clown Quilt
hand template
D
reverse for
template F
(pale pink solid)

Naptime Clown Quilt
eyeball and nose
template
(nose: red solid
eyeball: blue solid)

attach to section B

Naptime Clown Quilt
hat
template
section A
(reverse for other side of hat)

(1 green solid, 1 red polka dot)

Naptime Clown Quilt
hat
template
section B
(reverse for other side of hat)

attach to section A

Naptime Clown Quilt
eyelid
template

(mauve solid)

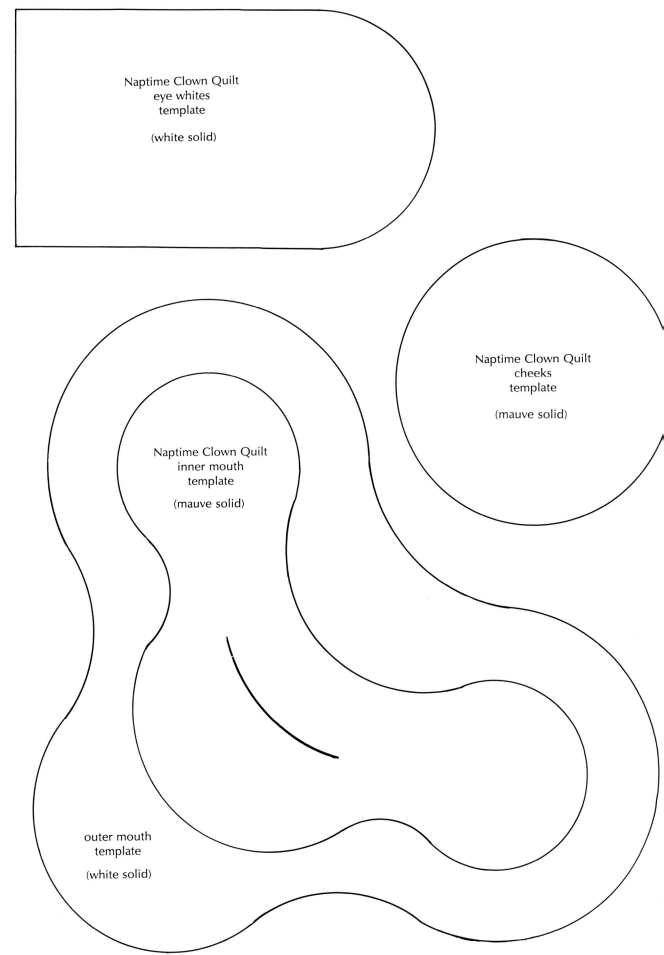

Naptime Clown Quilt
eye whites
template

(white solid)

Naptime Clown Quilt
cheeks
template

(mauve solid)

Naptime Clown Quilt
inner mouth
template

(mauve solid)

outer mouth
template

(white solid)

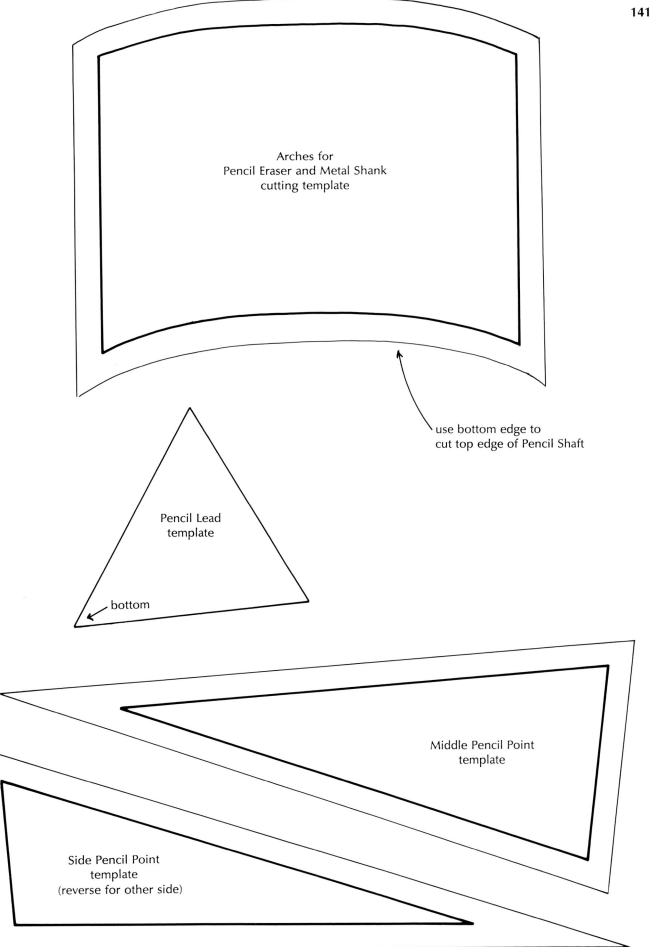

Arches for
Pencil Eraser and Metal Shank
cutting template

use bottom edge to
cut top edge of Pencil Shaft

Pencil Lead
template

bottom

Middle Pencil Point
template

Side Pencil Point
template
(reverse for other side)

Index

About the Authors

Anthony Jacobson is an award winning graphic designer. His love of fabrics and quilting started at the age of ten when he made his first quilt under his grandmother's watchful eye. Scores of quilts later, he now lectures to quilting organizations, and his original quilt designs have appeared in numerous shows and exhibitions, including a one-man show. Many are in private and corporate collections across the country.

Jeanne Jacobson is an interior designer with a bachelor's degree from Iowa State University. She has worked in both commercial and residential design, and uses her minor in art history to bring a variety of styles to her work. As a home seamstress she uses her sewing skills for home dec as well as garment construction.

Their collaboration began in Des Moines, Iowa in 1988. They now reside in Lansdale, Pennsylvania where they receive a great deal of help with their quilting from two American short-hair felines, Irene and Minnie.